It Just Is…

Dave Bull

It Just Is…

DISCLAIMER

What you read on the following pages is the opinion of the author and is not intended to malign any religion, ethnic group, organisation, company, gender, sexual orientation or individual. The views of the writer are his own, and (clearly) do not in any way reflect the views of anyone important. Furthermore, they do not necessarily reflect the views of the people who live in the author's neighbourhood, city, province, country, continent, hemisphere, planet, star system, galaxy, or universe of origin – including his friends…

Please also note that the fact the piece is written in English is in no way meant to malign other languages or linguistic ethnicities, nor to malign those who are illiterate or visually impaired and thus are unable to read the stuff he's written.

And… the individual letters, words, and punctuation marks involved had no option but to be placed onto the pages and in the order the author put them in. Whether they are in the right place cannot be blamed on individual letters, commas and the like..

Any spelling or grammatical errors are totally the responsibility of the schools the author attended and the educational system of the late seventies and early eighties in general.

The author takes no responsibility for his actions and opinions and holds his parents, siblings, other relations, friends and neighbours culpable for anything that may at first (and second) reading appear unsuitable.

No animals, or any other living things, (apart from trees - which we waited to die of old age…) were harmed during the making of this book

CONTENTS

	Acknowledgments	i
1	We Leave Our Brains At The Airport	1
2	It Just Is	3
3	Ready…?	7
4	January 2010	9
5	Finding your way…	15
6	Speaking another language …	29
7	(Not) keeping up with Lucy…	47
8	The day the Brits got on the council	55
9	The paperwork and the mess…	69
10	Of course I've read it…	83
11	When a melon just isn't enough…	93
12	Getting friendly with the locals…	103
13	The art of waiting…	119
14	When things go wrong…	131
15	Mrs Jones meets The Guardia…	143
	An overview	159

ACKNOWLEDGMENTS

To everyone who told me to,
'stop talking about it and get on with it'
– I owe you all x.

And to Suzanne Manners who dropped everything (not
literally) and dotted the i's and crossed the t's (literally) to
make this book somewhat readable.

To everyone else who offered encouragement
– you know who you are. x.

1 WE LEAVE OUR BRAINS AT THE AIRPORT

Something happens to us when we have made the decision to move to Spain and more specifically, buy a property there. At what other time in our lives do we make, possibly the biggest financial investment of our life based on a three day inspection trip in the back of a mini bus (taking as 'gospel' the word of Simon, our sales rep' who is sitting up front working out the commission before you've got to your hotel).

Ok some of us didn't buy that way but I can pretty much guarantee you that if you weren't with Simon helping him get closer to buying a BMW, then you made your own way over and 'had a look around for a bit.' We've all done one or the other and for some reason, sane rational, normally sensible people, will do something that we now think of as 'mad' but at the time would have probably done the same (some of us did).

Although most expats have settled happily in Spain, others have put their life savings into a soon to be completed property only to see the construction company go bust and all their money disappear. Others have built illegally either because the lawyer they employed was hopeless (we'll come to that) or they were told by fellow expats that they'd 'get away with it.'

Brits already living in Spain have a saying, that when people come over to live 'they leave their brains at the airport'; usually not realising that most of us could just as easily be put into that category too at some time or other.

It all sounds like doom and gloom, but it isn't. Many people have bought a property in Spain and lived happily ever after…even the married ones (well sometimes, but I'll get to that too a little later).

However, when my family and I first arrived we were taken to the middle of nowhere and then a bit further. Up a farm track to a tidy little farmhouse standing in about three acres. It had no running water and no mains electricity – although the salesman assured me that it would be connected 'very soon' – and was about forty years old. At the back of the kitchen I found a stack of car batteries that powered the naked bulbs in all the rooms. The price was €75,000, all that we had – and we put a deposit down on it. Fourteen grand's worth of deposit. Why? I've no idea what we were thinking at the time but, fortunately, thanks to an expat who was wise in the ways we managed to shift the deposit onto another house. Still miles from anywhere but at least we could have a wash.

2 IT JUST IS

The property boom in Spain lasted from 2001 until 2006 and in that time house prices went up by about 300% - and we Brits couldn't get enough of it. We poured into Spain like a friendly invasion, (an infantry in sandals and socks) and snapped up the houses, built or not, in preparation for the good life. But no-one, in all that time, seems to have learnt a thing until recently. No matter how many of us came to Spain: we believed whatever we were told. 'The lawyer says it's ok' or 'no you just do it illegally and if they catch you they fine you a little bit'. I know of people warned not to buy certain properties because so many who had were having trouble getting them declared legal, and still they bought.

Why after a couple of years weren't more stories coming out of Spain warning buyers to be careful (especially when choosing a lawyer) because of all the incredible, and ongoing, stories about buying a house in Spain? In my experience it seems that we either didn't want to believe any bad news or it was the 'it-won't-happen-to-me' syndrome.

Don't get me wrong, there are an awful lot of decent estate agents working the right way and looking after their customers, but during the boom there were an awful lot more looking after themselves...

Many of us also bought on the urbanisations – paying top dollar to live on an estate with properties half the size of the one we had left at home and the sort of quality that comes

3

when you build in a hurry or after a war. But we lapped it up with only minimal complaint to have the opportunity to 'live the life'. Some just accept, with a shrug, that nothing is going to be done about the fact that the builder didn't bother putting the waste pipe into the sewer and left it to fill your basement…oh well, at least it's sunny & we're in Spain!

I guess that is it. We are willing to accept less and do things the hard way to live the way of life that is on offer in Spain. Whether it's because of the language barrier, the laid back life, or the cultural differences (or all three) I don't know – it just is. And that's the best way to be in Spain, accept everything as it is and don't ask why on earth they do this or that, it just is.

I moved to Spain with my family at the end of 1999 and, although my marriage didn't work out in the end, I've gone on to enjoy my life as a single parent looking after my son Mitch, who was seven years old when we arrived here. Along with Meg the mongrel, the indomitable Mrs. Jones, Zammo (Mitch's best friend Jose who bears an uncanny resemblance to the Grange Hill character), and a host of other 'interesting' people we've had some fun, and this book was written during 2010; one of the most enjoyable (and interesting) years that we've had so far.

I'm now a full time writer, in one form or another, (but basically still a pie seller - my last job in the UK), having learnt my trade over the last ten years writing for several publications and, at the time of writing, publishing my own magazine for expats and working as the editor of an expat newspaper.

At first I hated Spain and the expat life and having sold the hire car business that I bought when I first arrived, I went back to the UK to work, commuting back to Spain twice every month. That was the turning point for me. When the work finished in the UK I thought that it was about time I gave Spain, and life as an expat, a proper go. Any country that considers changing lanes on a roundabout a serious offence but allows you to buy a chainsaw from Aldi has got to be worth looking at… so I threw myself into learning the language and integrating into the Spanish way of life. And I'm so glad I did. I don't want to get too sentimental, and I know in other 'expat living' books they drone on about their 'super Spanish friends', but I have made some good Spanish friends (and met some total tossers too). But when you speak the native language, you find the key to really 'living the life' in Spain; it opens up a whole new world and it is from this perspective that this book is written. It's not about knocking the Spanish (or the Brits) or Spain (I could write just as much about France…that would be a big book), but a tongue-in cheek look at life in Spain – warts an' all with some helpful stuff (if you're thinking of 'making the move') too.

As I say, this book covers a year of my life during 2010, and what a year! *Me and Mrs Jones* features typical expat experiences and not so typical ones that we face when living as a foreigner. My life is no more interesting than anyone else's - it's just that I've chosen to write about it. All of the stories and events that you'll read about really happened; just the names have been changed (unless they were guilty).

And let me state right now that although my romantic life is possibly less than successful at times, if I've learnt nothing else, I've learnt one thing about women…nope, it's gone again…

Daily life in Spain guarantees surprises; whether it's a local Mayor getting busted for taking a back-hander or a Benidorm Frank Sinatra tribute who is so old he can't quite get his leg up to do 'the kick' but still gamely carries on. And we love it.

Some people may recognize themselves, or indeed someone they know, in the pages of this book. Let me assure you now that if I've offended anyone, all I can say is…lighten up…

'Driving over Lemons' it ain't…

Dave Bull

3 READY…?

'What's it like living here then…?' how many of us expats have heard that? For those of you thinking of joining us 'living the life' let me tell you of all the tough bits about it so that you can make an informed and balanced judgment on whether to spend the rest of your days in your stealth taxing, knife-wielding politically correct island in the Atlantic or here in the sun, by a beach.

If you're reading this and considering immigrating to Spain, where do I start on preparing you for what might be a revelation or even a spanner in the works for your plans on cutting the apron strings and leaving the motherland?

For a start, I must tell you about the Coffee.

El café is one of the most important things involved in daily life – comes a close second behind breathing here – and something you'll need to adapt to if you are to survive the first few months. You see, you will need to get at least six or 7 cups down you a day and you must spend at least an hour over each one – while conversing with another of a like mind - and be in no rush to leave should something else have been pre-arranged, such as a wedding.

Along with building up a strong resistance to caffeine you will also need a bit (and I mean a fair bit) of stamina to spend the day on the beach or around the pool. It gets so hot here that at times we even have to find some shade or dip into the sparklingly blue (and clean) Mediterranean to cool off if we intend to try and endure the whole day lying down. The consumption of liquids is again necessary too – but we do not have the coffee at this stage of the day – we have to pour copious amounts of cold beers or cheap (and superb) local wines.

Then there are the Fiestas – don't start me on them. Too late. There is not a month (that should be day) goes by that there isn't something somewhere that the Spanish find to celebrate. There's even one to commemorate the birth of the donkey on which Mary bounced into the stable…. we expats feel obliged to attend these late night parties if only to placate our native hosts who will insist on pouring yet more liquids (and enough food to feed a teenage Panda) down your throat until the sun begins to rise and it's time to get ready for work.

How do the locals treat us? They only go and remember your name the next time you are around and insist on you joining them for more food and/or drink (no matter what the time of day or night), whether you have the time or not…nightmare!

Oh, and finally, unlike those amongst you who may come here for only a few days or a couple of weeks until you return home – we have to do this nearly every day. For most of the year it's a routine out here - we get up in the morning and there it is again, sunshine. Glaring and encouraging us to finish work early or throw a sickie and spend the rest of the day basking in it. Anyone reading this in the land of rain won't appreciate the sacrifices we make daily to live here…but if you think you're up to it – come on over….the water's lovely…and the beer, and the wine, and the tapas, and the people, and…

4 MONDAY JANUARY 4TH 2010

Another cigarette exits my packet. Then my lighter disappears. I am in Juande's cafeteria in the Glorieta Square, Santa Pola near Alicante.

Juan, the café owner and 'when I feel like it' waiter wanders off with a puff of smoke to chat with another customer at another table in this typically Spanish hostelry – and with my lighter.

I'm here because it's my escape. My bolt hole. A place to sit and write with a large coffee amongst good people – and where else can you sit all day and have a couple of coffees to interrupt the chat without getting a piercing look from the owner. Ok it will cost me a few ciggies during the day too (and probably a lighter) but it's a small price to pay when you're enveloped by what is best in Spain - the traditional and the cultural. Outside of the front door, the recently extended Glorieta Square leads to the impressive five hundred year old castle – and Juan's twin brother stands idly chatting with another local – with my lighter…

The noise inside is incredible as mostly housewives joust for their particular piece of gossip to be heard before and above all others. The rest of us raise our voices to be heard over the din, thereby increasing the overall volume that bit more. You'd think it'd be impossible to get any work done at all but for some reason I can get more done in a couple of hours (ok, maybe four…) in there than I can all day at home.

Juan and his wife Lolis have run the café for the past twenty-five years having converted it from a general store in 1983. Juan's parents had opened the shop in 1930 and ran it for the next 53 years, supplying the town with everything from light bulbs to Goldfish, in fact the front of the building appeared in the major Spanish feature film 'The man with the white umbrella' in 1959…no, I hadn't heard of it either.

Incidentally, if you should come to my part of Spain, specifically Santa Pola, I hope you get crabs. Fresh Santa Pola crabs at that – the best crustaceans around (apart from a bowls team I saw last week…they were good) and seriously good food. Good for your health, good to taste and, possibly more importantly, good for your pocket. However, this isn't a story just about crabs - that would be shellfish (sorry…).

We've all heard the story of the loaves and the fish where more than five thousand people were miraculously fed, with just five loaves and two fishes. If that was to happen today my mum could do it. She seems to be able to feed as many people as will show up - and the cupboards still remain full. Anyway, put the loaves and fishes story into a modern context and we'd probably just make a load of fish finger sandwiches. That's what this is about too really.

If there's one thing I've learnt since living in Spain it is the benefits of eating well, and especially fresh produce. As opposed to a reconstituted mash in a burger bar called a 'Seaman's Slice' or something.

Living in a fishing port means your seafood will be fresh. It's more than likely that it is just a few short hours since your chosen meal was swimming around wondering what was for dinner…and then realising…it was. That's how fresh it is. At the fish market (Plaza de Abastos) in the centre of town you'll find that day's catch displayed so that you can see the whole of the fish. Where I live the locals know their seafood and the vendors know what the locals want…good fish and the buyers will soon let the vendor know should the produce not come up to standard.

Local housewives will be along to natter, barter, natter a bit more and then argue some more about the price, before bidding the vendor a fond farewell…until tomorrow.

Mediterranean people live longer than the rest of us (a miracle if you've seen them drive) and those in the know tell us that it is not least because of their diet of seafood. The fact that they can smoke about 50,000 fags (each) every day and still curl their toes up years after us just endorses the argument. If you don't normally buy fresh fish, try it – you may be surprised. It's simple to cook and just as cheap as buying a slab of Salmon with three eyes from Buyeckistan or the like, and far tastier…unless eyes are your thing I suppose.

A walk along the prom, a cool beer and then buy your dinner. A little olive oil and garlic along with the fish in the pan – and you have it…delicious, trust me…I love Spain.

MONDAY JANUARY 25th 2010

After going head over heels (again) during the night I've decided I either need to get a new rug, or a different colour dog but although I've survived another week in Spain nothing seems to change but the reality is that everything changes, constantly, especially on an Urbanisation - but you just get so used to it; things that would make the hottest gossip at the front of the checkout queue back home hardly draws a raised eyebrow on the Urb's.

'Ave you 'eard?' is often followed by, 'so and so from the Brit bar ran off last night with the chef…'

Then… 'Really! So how's her husband doing?'

'He's opening at seven tonight.'

'Oh good.'

However, it doesn't take a certain type of person to live abroad, particularly Spain. In my experience, it takes a hell of a lot of different types of people to live in a place like this.

Having said all that - there are certain breeds that are to be found all over Spain – especially on the Urb's.

It's this type of person that you'll meet, work with and maybe even go out to dinner with (or possibly even run off with). You need to know what to expect (if you don't already) and perhaps you will find that you evolve into one of the Breed that exist on the Costa Blanca.

What we expats do for sure is to moan about the Spanish at times as I'm sure they do about us. However, I'll give the Spanish one thing (apart from having just about the best footy team in the world) and that is, they are honest. Now before you start complaining about the plumber telling you he'll turn up on Tuesday and actually coming four months later or the shopkeeper who says that the dress is definitely your size before you get home and try it on - realising that you look like you're smuggling potatoes. I'm talking about the serious stuff – when it really means something to them, they can be as blunt as the Derby forward line last season.

I say this not just to fill a few lines but because a good (Spanish) friend of mine recently celebrated her birthday and it had not been long before this that we had discussed the subject and how each of us celebrated them. To my surprise, Nicole (we'll call her that because that was her name…) told me that she never really did much on her birthday these days, much less get presents. I decided to make her next birthday a surprise by getting her something small but something that would perhaps mean something to her.

After deliberating for what seemed like days I decided in my wisdom that a watch was the answer – you see the irony..? A watch? She's Spanish and always late… Never mind. So that's exactly what I did and went and got the said prezzie – wrapped of course – and come the day I presented her with her, er, present.

Nicole thanked me profusely telling me what a good friend I was to think of her but…. actually, she didn't like it. I climbed back on the stool and sat there open-mouthed as she told me *all* of the reasons she didn't like it and thank you very much but could I change it?

I did. and I've changed it three times since….each time I get a little closer to what she's looking for - I'm sure we'll get there eventually… Whatever happened to getting the car cleaning kit for Christmas and telling Aunty Sue that it is just what you needed as you put in an (another) Oscar-winning performance – much more fun – I do it to our magazine photographer every year and then watch as he tries to appreciate a 'Limited Edition' Chinese Waterfall Clock (only another 4,449,000 were made)…

One more gem from Nicole…

When my mum recently visited she joined us for a meal and at the end of the evening, when mum could still drink Beefeater but no longer say it, Nicole commented that she was a very happy person…for such an old lady….

5 FINDING YOUR WAY…

SUNDAY JANUARY 31ˢᵗ 2010

What a January day. The sun is shining, the sky is blue and I'm sitting in one of Alicante's trendiest bars in the trendiest area, but just at the wrong time of day… Effigies of Tin Tin and Snowy and the Thompson Twins (not the 80's band) surround me - this is Captain Haddock's Bar. On the arm of Alicante port, this place is alive with music, laughter and life - buzzing with youthful sweat and expectation, but at night. Not, as usual, while I am here. Still, not a bad place to be; seagulls screeching and scrounging in the sun and the clink clink of yacht masts while well-dressed locals amble along looking relaxed and content. The odd Brit (easy to spot: football shirt, tattoo, shorts in winter, socks and sandals – and the men are as bad) stumbles along dragging a hot family behind in search of 'a bloody pint and some chips.'

I've escaped to the port but back on the Urb things are kicking off again, the personal trainer is back. Having left under a very dark cloud a year ago the Urb's very own Mr Motivator is back - minus the wife. Mr M vehemently denied any 'improper' behaviour with one of his attractive, Swedish, female, curvy clients and went back to the UK – chasing the wife – and bemoaning those who prejudged. Well that didn't work out and luckily Miss Sweden has allowed him to move in with her, and help look after the little one. Not sure where Miss Sweden's husband is in all this but was last heard of sending emails from a North Sea oil rig threatening to 'rip out Mr M's lungs and feed them to the fish...'

While I'm here though I really need to get a front page story finished for the newspaper about Triads. You see in my role as the editor I don't get to face much danger – the worst I get is probably a letter from 'annoyed – name and address withheld.' So when I decided to write an article about people-trafficking on the Costas - after receiving bagful's of letters concerning the presence of East European prostitutes on just about every roundabout in Spain, and Chinese DVD sellers outside of every bar - I thought nothing of it. My boss Ken, an ex-army major, ironically doesn't like confrontation and was worried that the Triads would be out to get us if we printed it and made me remove any reference that might incur the wrath of the 'Godfathers' of the orient.

His son Nick, who owns the newspaper, doesn't help either. He thinks he knows what he's doing with computers but has about as much success as a cow with a Rubik's cube. Each of our computers has problems with email. My 'Inbox' receives at least five hundred messages per day (of which about 490 are 'junk') so if I have a day or two away from the office I can return to well over a thousand emails to search through on my return. Having said that, this week it's stopped working altogether, which in a way is a blessing. Couple that with the fact that Ken's other son, Derek, has swapped my computer with his – 'because it's better than mine' – and now I don't have Microsoft Word, or any other word processor program. I also can't print anything because the printer can't be connected to my computer...according to Nick, and so here I am a journalist with a PC that can't print and with no way to read letters, articles or comments, or even with a means of communicating with anyone electronically – and I'm now writing this at home on a Friday after a week of working like this.

Still next week things will sort themselves out I'm sure.

I stopped off for a burger on the way home and felt that I should really congratulate Ronald for making something that tastes exactly like it sounds, have you tried the McWrap…?

Home and the kitchen's a mess…again. However, if you've not got a kid, my advice is to get one because watching kids, and especially teenagers, can be immensely rewarding…and hugely entertaining. Take Mitch, my seventeen year old son for example, and his mates of course, who all do the things I used to do at their age – and I thought I'd thought of it first too.

The problem at the moment is the frying pan; just recently Mitch has taken a liking to fried egg sandwiches for his breakfast which means the frying pan gets used, and left on the hob…for days. I've tried getting him to wash it up – but his argument, which is not bad actually, is that he'll use it again soon 'so what's the point?' It's hard to argue against….especially considering his bedroom looks like the last resting place for old socks and indiscernible plates of food. But then he is a teenage lad and if his room was tidy and ordered I suspect he'd be wanting matching curtains and cushions…and putting up posters of Shirley Bassey and ABBA.

It's great when the 'lads' come around for a barbecue though, bringing their egos (fully inflated) and boasting of how they plan to stay up all night drinking…

A couple of hours later and having cleared up the vomit they usually head home and we don't see them for a day or two. On nights out they'll all pile into our house and take up the two bathrooms to get ready. By the time they leave 'to meet some lucky girls' the dogs and I are high on the smell of testosterone and aftershave (Pico Riban from the market) which will deter any mosquitoes (and possibly Rhinos, judging by the strength of it). Once gone, the house is mine again and an early night…until the usual happens, Mitch will come home, sit on the bottom stair and begin shouting drunkenly,

'DAD…you ashweep? DAD! I'm home….DAD?'

It's at this point I snore loudly, roll over and think, 'fuck off…'

WEDNESDAY FEBRUARY 10th 2010

This week I had to return to the UK as my mum was having some serious blasting done at the Chemotherapy unit in Brighton so my son, Mitch, and I booked flights…cheap ones…

Apparently now one of the budget airlines wants us to carry our own bags to the plane. Yet another of their ideas to save money. But before you get carried away and say that it'll be good for the passenger because they'll save money -forget it. Because a spokesman from the airline informs us that they need to take these measure to 'keep prices competitive.' You'll notice he doesn't say to reduce prices but reading between the lines it's pretty clear that they'll be reducing costs and improving their profit margin while at the same time getting us to work for them- for free. How long before the pilot approaches you in your seat (a seat that you've actually brought yourself from the IKEA dining suite at home because it'll help keep prices competitive) and, noticing that you have a pile of tasty sandwiches on your lap, asks if you could offer some about the plane? 'And while you're at it…you could bring a bigger flask next time.' Soon it'll cost you a quid to spend a penny (that's a fact, apparently) and you'll have to check in yourself because there won't be one of those women (who look like they've been transferred in from the perfume counter at Boots) to take your ticket for you. If you enjoy your food that's gonna cost you more soon too as the airline plans to tax people for excess weight and I'm not talking about the baggage.

Flying used to be part of the holiday but today's 'budget' airlines (who seem to be the same airlines as before but without the 'meal' at halftime) have turned it into something you have to endure before you get to the fun bit.

But, I'm afraid, dodgy pricing doesn't stop with budget airlines – have you rented a car lately? There are now more add-ons than there are parts on the vehicle you're trying to rent. They'll give you a price on the net and you think 'hey, that's not bad at all' until you get here and they tell you that's just the price of the car – you now need to pay insurance, wheel cover, roof cover, extra driver cover and more.

'Need a baby seat sir? So that's you and the baby (possibly) coughing up.

It's at this point you start totting up the cost and look at the baby and wonder if he'll notice that he's strapped in firmly…in the boot.

This time last year car hire was so cheap that they almost gave you the car for the price of a packet of cigarettes but now they seem to have realised what the Americans have been up to for years (I don't mean bombing countries) and that's a shame. Ok, for the past few years it has been ridiculously cheap and all the extras were thrown in but now they've gone to the other extreme and are charging more if you plan to use the indicators. The fuel 'deal' also needs to be looked at, closely.. Pay for a full tank (which is about the same price as refueling a Boeing) and they tell you to bring it back empty – impossible, and they know it but I wish that just once someone would return their hire car to the airport and proceed to siphon the remaining fuel out of their hire car – because they've paid for it…

FRIDAY FEBRUARY 19th 2010

Mrs Jones, a Great Dane puppy has moved in. and apart from chewing everything in sight and falling off of the sofa (backwards) at an alarmingly frequent rate, she seems to be developing nicely. I'm not helped by the fact that my teenage son has many of the same clumsy traits as the puppy but I guess that's why they get on so well.

SATURDAY 20th FEBRUARY 2010

Not sure if it was deliberate but Mrs Jones managed to get me good and proper last night. While I slept she planted several of her 'aromatic landmines' next to my bed and then sat on the opposite side of them to me. At five am precisely she began barking as loudly as she possibly could. I woke up, startled, rushing over to her to see what the problem was only to discover her version of an IED with both feet. Jones? She wagged her tail and went back on the sofa, bless…

That evening Bertie and Wooshter (he did tell me his real name but, being Dutch, I kept coughing up phlegm every time I tried to pronounce it, it sounded like Wooshter though) called round.

Anyway, they are Jehovah's witnesses and regularly visited round the Urb' trying to sign up members to their particular brand of religion. I'm not for or against – if anyone wishes to believe, good luck to them – but I would refuse to wear those sandals…

Initially they called round about once a month, but as soon as I showed a glimmer of interest the visits became a bit more frequent – every week. I don't actually mind as I'll debate 'till the end of the world, resurrection and especially priests who will swear celibacy while bouncing a choir boy on their knee.

We've had some good chats, but (always) I get the impression that they are just about to try to get me to eat crisps or sacrifice the hamster or whatever it is you do to join. I just couldn't. I'm a coward and if one day a Spanish driver decides that actually, it's far more interesting looking at everything else but the road and the inevitable happens, i.e. I'm lying in the gutter oozing gallons of claret down the road. I want blood. I don't give a toss where it comes from but if that is what I need to survive then no God is gonna be able to convince me that going pale and looking like a wrung out dishcloth is what's best. Besides, I want presents at

Christmas, still. No, I think of myself as more of a Jehovah's Bystander…time for work.

SUNDAY FEBRUARY 21st 2010

Debbie, the man-hungry saleswoman, came into the newspaper office today and started hassling me. I've said 'no' so many times but Debbie does not give up easily – she's not after me physically, she wanted me to put my details on her friend's new dating website but I really didn't want to get involved, until that was she told me that it was full of single women, and there are hardly any men on it. I gave in but insisted that she put in all the details if she wanted me on there so badly. Off she went, returning frequently with questions about my favourite food and what chocolates I would buy my first date. Marmite sandwiches and Smarties are (apparently) not appropriate answers so Debbie said not to worry - she'd fill it out. I left her to it, not intending to ever do anything more with the website anyway.

However, by the time I got home I was curious about Debbie's efforts (on *my* behalf) on the dating site. So in the darkness of my bedroom, like a kid looking at porn, I checked out the website, all the while taking furtive looks at the closed door in case Mitch should walk in. If he caught me on a dating site my life would not be worth living – I can see him doubled up with laughter and refuse to give him the pleasure – so back under the duvet with the laptop.

Carefully I filled in all the boxes required for the search, the 'female' box obviously got a tick although the availability of 'other' alongside 'male' was a little worrying. Height? Build? Fat? Thin? I ticked all the relevant ones and hit the search button and off it went to find my true love.

You know when you open the front door and someone is standing there that you haven't heard approach – it frightens the life out of you doesn't it? Well that's how I felt as in the darkness supplied by a thick duvet up popped the face of my perfect match – Debbie from the office. I tried again several more times, changing the criteria with each go, but still the only person who came up was her. Conned, again.

Still, on the bright side, an old (female) school friend was flying over to stay in the area so who knows? She was a cracker at school.

When I'd gotten home earlier I'd had to give some poor bloke, who was lost, directions - it was our new postman…they change weekly out here. But asking directions from a Spaniard is a different matter altogether.

Have you ever been lost or perhaps not lost but you're heading off to visit friends - for a barbeque, or maybe it's that other little gem typical in Spain – the one that's comparable to the slap on the arse from the nurse when you first arrive in the world – going to find that widget for your new house that can only be bought in a small shop on the other side of Alicante. In a back street.

It's one of the great things about starting a new life, in a new place, with lots of other confused people. Because, as you haven't quite had time to grasp the language yet, you are reliant on the expertise of those of have been through this particular ordeal before you.

The problem comes when you find yourself hopelessly lost, or as my dad would say, just not where you should be, and you need to ask the directions of a native. You'll have thought at the time, and quite logically, that the wisest thing to do - now that you've found yourself in a bus lane, with a bus up your backside, and what looks like Bluto from Popeye in the driver's seat – would be to ask someone who lives locally. And, if your brain works like mine (occasionally) you would head for the wizened old fella on the bench, with the hat, the dog, and his trousers pulled up to his chest. TIP: trust me, I lived by this rule in the UK – if you get lost, ask an old boy (with a dog) whose waistband is rubbing his nipples and he'll guide you in better than mission control. The reasoning is obvious; if the gentleman is, shall we say, in the autumn of his life, and the guy has a dog – he is probably local. Just what is needed at a time like this. But no, this man is Spanish and this is a mistake I made, time after time, until it finally dawned on me.

You see, it's a bit like how they drive, and walk. Nothing exists if it's not directly in front of them. The times I've clattered into the back of someone as they've stopped directly in front of me (for no noticeable reason) and *I* end up saying sorry! It's the same with driving, ever been behind a car that has just spotted a handy parking spot for their Seat Ibiza? The fact that you could get an aircraft carrier into the gap is irrelevant as they slam the car into reverse and two bright white lights start heading towards you, fast. And don't get me started on hill-starts…if you pull up within about ten feet of their bumper when they stop on a hill – beware! More than once I've found a car resting on top of the front wheel of my scooter because they didn't catch (find?) the clutch in time.

But - I digress - what I'm trying to say is that for a nation rich in history and famous explorers, who helped create one of the biggest empires ever seen, they are absolutely crap at pointing you in the direction of, say, the central post office. What they will do is tell you where it used to be, and then decry the local town hall for moving it and costing local people jobs etc. Helpful if you're into social politics but not if you're trying to buy a stamp.

Another thing they'll do is send you off to the end of the road – to ask someone else…

'Just go all the way to the end of this road…' they'll say, as your excitement mounts at the prospect of reaching your own particular Holy Grail,

'and then when you reach that church…'

'Yes..?'

'Ask again…'

So you do, and like a human pinball you bounce around the town until you finally arrive at wherever it was you needed to be….and it's shut for lunch…

So is it really any wonder they drive so fast? There's such a small window of opportunity to get anything done (with

Spanish opening hours) in the morning (especially for the unsuspecting expat) that unless you belt around town with screeching tyres and follow the bus through the changing lights ('they were still amber-ish') you don't have much of a chance of making it.

Many times, when I used to deliver rental cars, I would ask a local where a particular street was, only for him to scratch his head, before shaking it, and giving me a (truly) regretful 'sorry.' I'd then find the street I was looking for, next to theirs.

Compare that to any British town or village and you will damn near get a grid reference from a local who will, (in my village they did…) not only give you directions, but also fill you in on any developments in that household, whether you wanted to know or not.

I'm not saying the Brit way is correct or even better, because when you think about it, the Spanish have probably got it right. When you ask them why they don't know the name of a street a hundred metres from their front door the answer is always the same,

'Because I don't use that road…'

They don't feel the need to know…they worry about their immediate vicinity – whether walking, driving or living - and that's about it. It's either that, or knowing the Spanish sense of humour, they know exactly where we want to go…but wouldn't it be fun to see a load of 'Guirees' flying around the province, glancing at their watches and saying 'grassius' every time they get sent to the other end of the street to ask again…

TUESDAY FEBRUARY 23rd 2010

I arrived at the newspaper office and someone had kicked a cable, so none of us had email again. Well, that was Derek's diagnosis of our problems as he shut his door and left us to it. Ken, (the boss's dad) is away in Barcelona, Nick (the boss) is in the Costa del Sol and the rest of us were trying to put a newspaper together with what seemed like bits of string and brown paper (ok, white paper – but you see my point?). Still it kept it interesting, if not functional.

Derek, the designer/photographer went out to take some photos at one of the local football matches today where he met up with my mate, and fellow photographer, Harvey. At this point I should point out that Derek is to photography what I am to ballet – if I've got the shoes it doesn't exactly make me Dame Margo now does it? For the whole ninety minutes Derek was having problems with his camera – nothing was in focus – until Harvey pointed out that the 'A' on his equipment stood for 'Aperture' not 'Auto' as Derek had thought…

Also this week, a rival radio station blocked the signal of the one owned by the newspaper by broadcasting porn on the same frequency, and all five sales girls had a row with Nick and the atmosphere is, shall we say, emotional. Two companies came in demanding the money they are owed by the absent Nick. Sarah, my colleague, and I have been asked to work more hours for the same wages. Oh yes, and two ex-staff have been in, dropped off writs, and are now suing him…told you it was interesting.

More work appeared on my desk when I found out that March the 8th (which is coming up soon) is International Women's Day and you know what that means…somewhere in the calendar there will be an International Men's Day – and we're no good at that sort of thing. Let's be honest chaps, we don't really give a monkey's about any other 'special' day; Father's Day, Mother's Day, Mother-in-law's Day (yup, 4th Sunday in October), Sheep Day (Wales/New Zealand only). And of course we're programmed (unlike the ladies) to forget any other important day on the calendar such as anniversaries or the nephew's probation or something. So giving us our own day is a pointless waste of time – because we won't be raising money for causes, running around helping others and the like. No, we (if, by some act of God, we actually manage to remember the day) will go out and get bladdered….or is that just me..?

The women, I know, will be doing useful things like organising Fetes, social gatherings and generally making the most of the day, which by the end of it will have raised a considerable amount for charity and good causes and highlighted awareness of needy causes. As it says on their website,

'(The day) is a global day celebrating the economic, political and social achievements of women past, present and future.'

However, ours (November 19th) will come and go and we'll remember the 20th more because of the hangover. Whoever decided we should have one can have it back. We don't need one, just because women have one someone feels obliged to make the men have one and we don't want it. The women have had their day every year since 1919 but no one introduced the IMD until *eighty* years later and there's a very good reason for that....none of us blokes were bothered about having one, or is that just me...again?

When it comes to things like this, and shopping, we're just different animals. For example, the other day I went to the supermarket and bought some essentials as the fridge was empty once again. (my son is in and out of the fridge so often that my neighbours thought that I had a strobe light in the kitchen...). Anyway, in front of me in the queue was a middle-aged woman buying her food, and very nice it was too; several cheeses (of varying vintage, and smell no doubt) some pates, meats, a basket of fresh vegetables and some fresh fish. Oh, and a very nice red wine. I pictured the scene; a table set and the feast laid out amongst candles while the wine glasses chink to the background of light jazz. But, judging by the look on her face, she was doing the same as she looked at my dinner; a pork pie a tin of beans and some Jelly Tots...you see, we're different. Another example would be when I went to the hairdresser (for a cut) and she said my hair was damaged and I would need some conditioner. 26€ worth of conditioner! How on earth can women afford to live? I could have spent that on something shiny, like a gadget.

And anyway (I'm not letting this go am I?), why is their day in the middle of spring, just as the weather is warming up and fluffy bunnies are gently bouncing in meadows (bear with me…), and ours is lumped in the middle of winter; when it's dark about half an hour after you've got up and anything with any sense is hibernating?

When I got home Reg, my neighbour, needed some help calling the electricity company because he'd been cut off, again. Reg doesn't 'do languages' so I gave them a call for him – and told him it was about time he DID languages, for his own sake.

Maybe you've not lived here long, or perhaps you've lived here a while…whatever…it doesn't really matter but if you're struggling to learn Spanish – which type of Spanish are you struggling with? Do you know, or even care? You should because there are *eight* official languages in Spain and you need to know which one you are mispronouncing. Add that to all the other languages from Europe that you'll hear on these shores and it's no wonder the teenagers have invented their own dialect, grunting.

Ok, brace yourself…

The national language of Spain is Castilian but there are seven other provincial languages that are officially recognised. During Franco's time these local languages were outlawed but since his death there has been an almost fanatical resurgence in the use of them – sometimes to the point where Castilian has been excluded, even here in my town of Santa Pola that has happened. The government is trying now to redress the balance but the provinces are tad slow in reacting.

So what are they?

Castilian or Castellano, which is internationally recognised as Spanish or Español, spoken by about 75% of the population and understood by virtually all. Worldwide it is estimated that in excess of 350 million people in 44 countries use Castilian and its regional variants as their first language.

Catalan, Catala and Valencian Valenciana, (from my area) is a group of languages that is spoken by an estimated 10 million people, with around 7 million using it as their primary language, plus numerous people who don't want you to understand what they are saying. Geographically, it is spoken in the provinces of the eastern seaboard; Catalonia (official language), Valencia (Valenciana, official language) and the Balearic Isles (Balear Catalan, official language) as well as part of Aragon. It is also spoken in Andorra, France and Sardinia and is the 21st most commonly spoken language in Europe (out of 56)

Galician, Gallego or Galician is really a dialect of Castilian, with some Portuguese influence, and is the language of the north west of Spain where it is spoken by 3 million people. It's a language with a long literary history.

Basque, Euskera, is the language of some 600,000 in the three Basque provinces of Alava (Araba), Biskaia (Biskay) & Guipuzkoa and the northern part of Navarra, as well as about 100,000 in the Pyrénées-Atlantiques region of France. This ancient language is unrelated to any other European language and understood by very few so it was probably invented by teenagers.

Asturian or Asturiano, Bable is only spoken by about 450,000 people in the northern province of Asturia, with just 100,000 using it as their main language.

Extremaduran or Extremeño is an ancient language that some 200,000 regularly use; it is a Leonese dialect of Castilian.

Other indigenous languages spoken in Spain include languages such as Aragonese (about 30,000 speakers), Fala (10,000 speakers) and Occitan (which has no figures but it must be at least two…?)

Now wasn't that interesting…

6 SPEAKING ANOTHER LANGUAGE…

SATURDAY MARCH 6th 2010

No more blind dates. Last night it was Zenka (from somewhere with a funny alphabet) and unfortunately, she needed a shave more than me.

Oh well, it was Mitch's birthday so we were taking the motorbikes to the track to have some fun racing against other riders (and each other) around Albacete circuit.

As ever it was an early start and we were on the road by half past seven with Mitch sleeping fitfully in the front seat beside me. I say fitfully…he woke every ten minutes or so, ate a sandwich, and fell back to sleep. Leroy, who sat in the back seat, regaled me with stories of his childhood (he's seventeen…) and how he could never ride a motorbike after he fell off his bicycle head first into a wall. Although that explains a lot about him I was struggling to stay awake and started adding up just how much this day out was costing…me.

With circuit fees and insurance taking the best part of three hundred euros, I'd filled our pick-up with fuel for the journey (another seventy euros) and bought 150 litres for the bikes – about another 180 euros, which took the total to well over five hundred – for a day out. And that was without eating or drinking or buying something from the bike shop…that we wouldn't need but would buy anyway.

Still, by the time we arrived at the race track we were buzzing with excitement and adrenalin, and the combined noise and smell of over fifty other bikes getting ready put a grin on our faces.

By the time we had got our bikes, and ourselves, ready quite a few other racers were already out on the track. Adrenalin seriously flowing by now, and a heartbeat so strong and rapid that I could feel it in my chest, we pulled out of our box and onto the pit lane with Mitch going in front of me. The marshals let him go fairly quickly while I had to wait for the traffic to decrease but once I got on the track I took it steady, expecting to come up behind my son after every corner. But I couldn't see Mitch anywhere, strange.

As I came around a wide left-hander on my second lap - I saw him, being carried into an ambulance while his bike (what was left of it) was carted away on a truck. I can't tell you the feeling of seeing that and knowing that there was nothing I could do but go around the rest of the lap – which I did in record time.

I drove the bike straight to the medical centre and just dumped it outside. Mitch wandered out with his arm in a sling, and a note telling him which hospital to go to…suspected broken wrist, he was lucky.

We spent the next three hours, firstly finding the hospital and then finding the accident department where we waited, in our leathers, for the medics to confirm his injury and then plaster his arm up to the elbow.

And that was it; we drove home with me thinking about saying goodbye to over five hundred euros to spend precisely three minutes forty two seconds on the track and three hours plus at the hospital. Oh, and not forgetting the damage to the bike…just a tad over six hundred euros. The organisers asked if I wanted to attend the spit-roast, which was kind but the way the day had gone I wasn't sure if we'd be eating crackling or watching a couple of premier league players, well, nuff said, I think. Looking on the bright side and as my mum would no doubt say (always turning things into a positive) 'well at least you had a change of scenery…'

However, for that money I could have flown to see the Pyramids in Egypt for the weekend (with a 'friend') now, that would be a change of scenery…

A night out should have helped make things at least feel better…wrong.

SUNDAY MARCH 7th 2010

Oh I didn't did I? I woke up and my head felt like someone was inside banging a saucepan with a hammer. Why? I had no idea but the 'several' pints the night before can't have helped. I'd also done something I would regret, and soon.

You remember when we were younger and you put your tongue across the terminals of a battery? You knew it was gonna be painful but you still did it for some reason. Well last night I did the romantic equivalent…I kissed Kate. Now at this point I would like to point out that Newton was correct with his theory of everything having an equal reaction because the more I seem to get to know a woman, the less I seem to understand…or is that just me?

Back to last night, Kate was a friend who wrote for my magazine. She'd been after me for a while but it wasn't that flattering as each week she'd phone up and tell me that she'd 'finally' met a great bloke. Followed two days later by another call to say 'great bloke' wasn't answering his phone.

'Have you shagged this one already?' I'd enquire, to which the answer was always the same.

'Yes – but this one's different.'

So far I'd managed to resist her attempts at romance but last night, aided by Heineken, Kate became quite attractive to me. I knew at the end of the night when she asked for a kiss that it was a bad idea but a decision had to be made. In between burps and hiccups I managed to rationalize that it was a great idea to kiss her, so I did. Then I staggered home having forgotten all about it and pretty much the rest of the evening actually.

SUNDAY MARCH 7th 2010 10.02am

The text messages from Kate were a little bit worrying to say the least. She suggested a day out with her and her three year old son followed by a DVD and some supper later. Help me.

SUNDAY MARCH 7th 2010 10.19am

I felt even sorrier for myself as I lay on the sofa and constructed a tactful reply along the lines of last night being a one-off and it'd ruin our friendship.

SUNDAY MARCH 7th 2010 10.24am

That was when the bunny really got put in the pan because the next text back accused me of being a 'Gigolo who can't control himself...'

I didn't reply and thought a couple of days would see things calm down. This, as you will see, just proves that I know bugger all about women.

SUNDAY MARCH 7th 2010 11.43am

Still, the day was young and I'd plenty to do (including keeping out of Kate's way) although I was thinking a long sleep on the beach might help when the doorbell went. Sweat immediately broke out on my forehead at the thought of Kate being on the other side of the door. But, fortunately, it was some people who I knew would take my mind off of the predicament.

The 'Witnesses' are back, Bertie and Wooshter came by to discuss evolution. I commented that I thought it was one of the best cars Mitsubishi have made but it didn't quite translate. Actually I think it may have translated to 'I want to shag you mother and eat your kids' judging by the look they gave me, but being 'children of God' they forgave me pretty quickly and the chat returned to monkeys and fish. It got quite good at one point when they conceded that we could have come from monkeys but seemed satisfied that they were right when I couldn't give them a breakdown of how it all exactly happened after the big bang. Although I'm sure they were in agreement with me when I argued that when God said 'all men are equal'…he didn't mean the French.

All the while I'd been talking Mrs Jones had been inside the house playing with my son and his mates. When I say playing - I mean eating, as the kids had decided they'd had enough and were going to watch telly. The trouble was nobody told Mrs J and she continued to dive from sofa to sofa - mauling flesh as she landed on each of them. The screams seemed to distract Bertie and Wooshter until a hushed silence descended. I'd just managed to get my God-fearing friends back on track when from the lounge my son shouted,

'bad news dad – she's eaten your Pamela Anderson fitness video…'

With Bertie and Wooshter gone, I got out on the motorbike and headed for the big city…Alicante, to find a café.

She's out here somewhere, gotta be. It'd finally dawned on me that the great love of my life was not going to be found knocking on my door with religious offerings or not. Or even 'accidently' dropping her groceries (let alone anything else) in front of me, any time soon. So what to do? Back to basics, I thought, and regressed to the hunter/gatherer mode of our ancestors by getting out there and looking for one. A mate.

SUNDAY MARCH 7th 15.00pm
El Albergue Bar, ALICANTE
Here's one now, opposite me, in the cafe that I've decided (after much consideration) to start my hunting in. I'm mixing with (drinking the same type of coffee as) the

young and successful who spend their Sunday mornings perusing the Sunday papers while dressed in their best. My hoody and shorts ensemble is possibly not my best option but it's too late to do anything about it now and anyway the woman sitting opposite is a possible candidate for the next Mrs Bull; attractive, slim, and on her own by the look of it. However, she is going through a bowl of nuts like a hungry chicken, pecking at farmyard seed – something we might have to look at if we're to have a future.

Whoa, hold on, because behind her bobbing head I can see a serious candidate. Ok, we haven't met yet but don't underestimate the depth of my shallowness because on looks alone – I can hear wedding bells. She's about the right age (under retirement), has no rings on her fingers and hasn't stopped laughing with her friends. Nice. I give her my seductive look, the one I've been practicing but if I get it wrong it looks like I've got trapped wind. She smiles back! I keep up the trapped wind grin as her smile broadens – and she's looking at me. Correction that should be looking through me, as over my shoulder I hear another voice, a friend sends her best wishes and invites her for a coffee in the week. Great.

Hang on though; her mate's not bad either. Dark hair, brown, eyes, olive skin, a traditional Spanish beauty with the only obstacle being the four kids that are hanging off of her, and the old man sitting next to her reading the paper. I turn back around to see the other one heading for the loo and now that I can see all of her I realised that while from the waist up she has film star looks, from the waist down she is Danny De Vito. Shame.

The nut woman is still pecking away like a good 'un so I turn my attention to the passers-by and take a straw poll – out of the next fifty women I see I wonder, on looks alone, how many I would actually want to spend some intimate time with? (I told you I was shallow). I'm worried I've become too fussy and this could be a way of finding out. Before I can start though a new waitress emerges onto the terrace and at first glance she could be a 'possible' but then the jaw-slapping technique of chewing her gum and the seven facial piercings are a bit of a put off.

Five out of the fifty I counted would make me happy, I reckoned. However, out of that fifty a good majority would have needed a flu jab to get through the winter and would have probably preferred to knit anyway. The rest were pretty much regular people – just not my type of regular people. Am I too fussy or is the demand greater than the supply? There's definitely a shortage of women because of the five that I would have liked to have spent some time with, all five were with their fellas. So where do they go, the single, available, and yes, if necessary, desperate? Where should I go to find them? Unless I find out, and soon, I guess I'll have to persevere like this, and work on the trapped wind. Having said that a total babe has just entered my life, well sat at the next table anyway. No rings, no bloke and a flirty smile. This one has it all…but, she smells like the cosmetics counter in Boots and on closer inspection, while she is obviously good looking, she has managed to get so much make up on her face I'm surprised he head doesn't tip forward – she must have strong neck muscles (which could be a plus) but her 'scent' is making me dizzy from ten feet so I guess that rules her out too…

I left, but before I did, I had a heated discussion with the locals about how bad they thought us Brits were for not making the effort to learn their language. While they accepted that I was ok, as I argued with them in Spanish, they called my fellow countrymen and women 'lazy' for not 'trying hard enough.

But, I think it's time to stand up for my country and defend our ability (or lack of) to speak foreign languages. Forever, it seems, foreigners have bemoaned the Anglo's 'laziness' or 'disinterest' in speaking a foreign tongue when in fact the entire fault lies firmly at the feet of our fore-fathers. Drake, Raleigh, Cook, Dr Livingstone and Homer Simpson have reached out to the four corners of our little planet and spread the English language far and wide, so much so that it is the number one idiom in the world, (ok, a lot of people speak Chinese but most of them live there and if not, they are concentrating on a menu or selling plastic footballs...). Us Brits are at a distinct disadvantage when it comes to learning a foreign language – we don't need to but the rest of the world does need a second tongue (insert joke here ladies) and that is English. It is the language of business, commerce, movies and computers. Anyone wanting to get on in the world is told to learn English. Whether it's in the banks of Switzerland or your local McDonald's on the Costa Blanca, there is a need to speak English because an awful lot of your customers will be foreign. Not necessarily English, they could be Scandinavian, German, and Russian or, God forbid, French, but the one thing that they will have in common is a basic grasp of English.

We on the other hand don't know which one to learn unless we are going to live in one place such as Spain. But then comes along the next problem. Age. As we get older our ability to learn lessens – you've only got to try and transfer all your numbers from one phone to another, impossible, unless of course you hand it to a five year old who will configure your memory card, remove those annoying texts and hand it back to you within thirty seconds. We've not had it drummed in to us from an early age that it is important to speak another language because, as everyone knows, the rest of the world speaks English, and pretty well too.

How many times have you gone to practice your Spanish in a local bar and the waiter insists on talking in English so *he* can practice? I'm not saying we should give up and let the world come to us, far from it, it shows a great deal of respect to our hosts here in Spain if we at least make an effort to talk to them in the language of the country we are in.

There's no excuse as far as I'm concerned for the bloke who, having spent two weeks (or even living here) in Spain to fill his car up at the petrol station on the way into the airport, to then say to the guy behind the till, 'pump four mate….cheers!' (This happened on more than one occasion while I was there). Yes it's hard to pick up the whole grammatical suitcase of Spanish but surely, even a moron can learn 'Gracias' in two weeks…?

It's a question of respect, not a massive problem that you'll never be able to overcome. All I say to the rest of the world is, bear with us; it is different (culturally) for the Brits but on the flip-side if the 'pump four mate' guy is there at the same time as you….teach him a new word would you? 'Respeto' would be a great start and he could learn it while he's taking his socks off to count to 18…

And, as if learning Spanish wasn't hard enough already – they, like every other country have slang words and no matter how hard you try, you won't find them in any dictionary but they are frequently used by all generations and sexes.

To help you along your way I've put together some of the most useful(?) and common words and phrases that you may well hear your Spanish neighbour shouting.

First there's 'Casero' (ka-sayr-Oh) which means Landlord but also 'Casera', apart from a female landlord, is a soda that, mixed into red wine, makes tinto de verano, a light summer drink – which I can recommend. And as an adjective, casero means home-made. Then there's always the useful Chalado (cha-la-doe) which means crazy or nuts.

One word which sounds like what it means is 'Chapuza' (cha-poo-the) which means shoddy work and sounds like you should spit it out, literally. Another that you will definitely hear a lot is 'De puta madre' (day poo-ta ma-dray) which (not literally) translated means the dogs bollocks (it does where I come from).

'Entender' (en-ten-dare) is a tricky one as it can mean to be gay. However, the main definition of the Spanish word entender is to understand, so keep in mind that if someone at a bar asks you 'Entiendes?' it could just as likely be a reflection on your Spanish skills as an attempt to find out your sexual preferences.

'Guiri' (gEE-ree) is a foreigner in Spain, especially an Anglo-Saxon or northern European foreigner but this word can be as affectionate or as disparaging as the speaker intends to make it…if they're snarling I think you can take it as offensive.

Anyone resident in Spain can't fail to have heard about 'Operación bikini' (oh-per-ah-the-own be-key-knee) which is the Spanish pre-summer custom of exercising, going on a diet, joining a gym, and other activities associated with wanting to look good in a bikini or swimsuit – mainly for women I believe although there's a few fellas around here…

Tener un rollo (ten-air Oon Roy-yo) is to have a fling or a casual sex partner – another phrase very useful out here…and, Topmanta (topp-mahn-tah) is a great name the Spanish use for an Illegal street vendor (usually African) who displays his wares (often pirated or counterfeited goods) on a small square of cloth – a manta/blanket. This they can have bundled up at a moment's notice and be legging it down the street before, or just as, the police appear.

Remember that many words in Spanish are dependent on the context they are used in so before you shoot out and ask the woman next door if she's gay…try and work it into a sentence that makes sense. Also don't forget that these are slang words and should really only be used in informal situations and not when you're addressing the bride's mother for example…

SUNDAY MARCH 14th 2010

'YOU'RE NEIGHBOUR THINKS YOU'RE HOT!' said the email. Unfortunately, Carmen, my neighbour, has cataracts and tends to call everyone 'Conjo' (if you don't know, you don't want to), so I had a feeling our romance was over before it'd begun. But why is it that I'm attractive to women…that I don't fancy?

Today was a prime example.

Sunday, and I was peeking through the curtains because an Indian ice cream lady (I kid you not) who takes her multi-coloured 'Softy' van up and down the coast, made her presence felt the other night. Since she found out that I'd separated from my ex, she'd been making very clear her (dis) honourable intentions towards me. As lovely as she is; she wears Day-Glo clothing during the day – headdress included and a different colour every day– and speaks with a strong cockney accent, I've had enough of women in my life that give stuff away in the back of a vehicle – know what I mean? So when at eight thirty - every night of the last week – she parked her ice cream van outside my flat and played her jingle, I had to hide and tell my son and his mates to tell her - I'm not in.

'Cost you an ice cream Dad.'

Now, let me advise right now that as a responsible parent you cannot let kids bribe you; it's a test of your authority and needs to be nipped in the bud straight away.

3 Choc-ices and a 99 later - for Mitch and his mates - and she'd moved on, and I came out of the toilet. Time to go out– it was getting too expensive staying in.

I headed for my favourite café, Juande's, and as I sat and wrote, inevitably the TV was on – loud, and as is popular in Spain there were about 150 adverts during the commercial break. My point– and I'm getting there ladies – is that one particular ad offers (I have no idea what they are called in English) pants for the 'larger' lady that basically pull everything inwards (if it's all squashed up how do you have a drink?) and once concealed under the outer clothes, gives the appearance of a much slimmer figure. What I want to know is this: if they work, and you are out on the pull one night (I'm not suggesting that all wearers behave this way…) isn't it a bit of a shock for the lucky fella?

I mean at the end of the night you slip back to his place for a coffee, get comfy, get intimate, and when he wakes up in the morning you look like you've eaten the pillows?

SUNDAY MARCH 14th 2010 15:53pm

Checking my emails I see I've got lucky, again. So far this month I've apparently won the Irish lottery (again) and am the beneficiary of 24.8million bucks – I just need to get it out of Africa…and untold fortunes that alleged soldiers in Iraq want to give me because they can't think of a better way of getting tons of gold out of Iraq – other than to contact a local magazine editor in Spain. And just this morning I was contacted by a Dr Dwanka (sounded like that) on behalf of the Rwandan government because they particularly need my bank account to deposit a load of cash - of which I'll be getting 35% - which I've worked out is a tad under 12 million US dollars. There are some really nice people about don't you think?

MONDAY MARCH 15th 2010 16:43pm

As I sip my steaming coffee a bleep from my mobile phone shows a text from Kate has just arrived asking what I'm planning to do with her and asking if I think I can just love and leave her like she's a 'piece of dirt'? It was a bloody kiss! That's all. The way she's going on now is as if I've got her pregnant, which I must add is impossible, unless sperm can now climb out of men's jeans and pierce (it must be said) a rather large and sturdy anorak that Kate wore that night.

MONDAY MARCH 15th 2010 16:58pm

My decision to let things quiten down has come across as if I'm ignoring her and my telling her to calm down and think about it is met with a tirade of abuse down the phone. I'm now thinking the best idea is to get her to hate me but bunnies and saucepans leap (or hop) to mind, so I'll ignore her.

I even started watching the dreaded TV to forget about Kate and on came the Spanish weather forecast. I had been joined by a Spanish friend, José, (I know…) and he launched into a (very) foul-mouthed tirade about Spanish weather forecasters and how they always get it wrong. He has a point. The Spanish weather forecasts are not the best in the world and with the guy (or girl) standing in front of half of Spain, blocking it off to half the population, they don't really help themselves.

'Look at bloody it!' he shouted above the TV, the stereo, the clientele, the coffee machine and the other telly, 'they always say that every day is bloody gonna be da bloody same! In England they tell you it is gonna rain at bloody half-past two and it bloody does!' I'd recently taught him the odd swear word and he tended to overuse them, a little, but it didn't seem like a good time to remind him that this is Spain and it usually is the same weather, most of the time.

As it turned out, it is (according to José) President Zapatero's and Franco's combined fault that the weather was wrong and the weatherman was a 'bloody son of a bitch' but whether the weather turns out to be right or wrong, you just feel better after a Spanish forecast than you do a British one. Theirs leaves you looking forward to a barbecue or the beach at the weekend. Ours will tell us how long we can spend outside before we catch some form of skin disease or whether hay fever sufferers should even bother getting up…

I've mentioned it to José once and I think I got away with it. But try and talk to a Spaniard about the Franco years, and they will, at best, give you a shrug and remind you that it was a long time ago. That's it, end of the matter as far as they are concerned but for someone interested in history, like me, it is a tad frustrating. Ok, so it was their war, their dictator and remains their history but I still want to know a bit more about it than the snippets I get from here and there.

What you do learn about those times is often tainted by loyalties and politics and can depend on who, if anyone, will tell it to you. Even then you have to take a fair amount of it with a fistful of salt; a good Spanish friend of mine who spent his childhood growing up under the shadow of the Franco regime told me how the town priest was one of the most revered men in his small pueblo. Whenever kids had to pass him in the street they were expected to kiss his hand before moving on. Another friend, who comes from the opposite end of the political see-saw, swears that it didn't happen like that at all and nobody even liked the priest anyway, let alone respected him. However, get the two of them together and they won't talk about it at all.

With the Spanish, the past is in the past. Gone. Take a look around Spain - how many castles, churches and other historic buildings do you see? Not many. Go to the UK and you can't get a fag paper between the National Trust preserved buildings and the English Heritage gardens, not to mention the incredible amount of listed buildings that have preservation orders – we like to keep stuff, they don't. Take the Mary Rose – the Spanish would have got that to the surface, taken one look at it, and burnt it for firewood whereas we'll spend zillions of pounds each year preserving it with what amounts to little more than a posh garden sprinkler.

So our (Brits) rich history is well recorded, not just on paper, but in the amazing number of ancient buildings and artifacts we have to visit and see. That's why the UK is inundated with obese Americans - in flowery shorts with wives called 'Barbara' and 'Junior' in tow - every summer but I guess every silver lining has a cloud. I can't for the life of me believe that in 150 years or so our descendants will be going stateside and having a guide show them around; 'this was a place where spotty kids used to sell meat in between two pieces of bread to fat people, and this was where spotty kids used to sell fried chicken to more, or possibly the same, fat people, and here – pizzas…', you get my drift?

However, in Spain, a country whose history is equally as rich as that of the UK or other European nations, what's gone is gone - new is good. They have, over the years, destroyed much of their heritage with no better reason than to chuck up a hotel or stick an EU-funded motorway on top of it. That's why they won't talk to me about it. And that's why Spain isn't catering for fat Americans every summer – it does make you think…

But I don't mind that they don't want to talk about the past to me – they were not good times and civil wars are the worst kind of conflict; pitching families against each other with brothers fighting brothers. They've had enough of talking about it and the pain that undoubtedly goes with it; for the older generation who remember the worst of it. No, as I say, it's their history and I'm the guest here, and anyway the Spanish have a great way of dealing with anything that is a problem…just pretend it doesn't exist – works for them.

TUESDAY MARCH 23rd 2010 12:13pm

Talking of trying to ignore people…I've woken up to discover that Kate has been text messaging again and it's not getting any better. Now, apparently, I should have thought of the damage I was doing instead of thinking with my dick and just getting what I wanted... it was just a kiss for chrissake!

TUESDAY MARCH 23rd 2010 12:37pm

My appeal for common sense falls on deaf ears as she (once again) reminds me how strongly she has always felt for me (conveniently forgetting the once-a-weekers who have been much more intimate than me) and that I should have somehow resisted the temptation when it came to the kiss.

TUESDAY MARCH 23rd 2010 12:49pm

Oh boy...so I agree. 'Yes, you're absolutely right and I should have thought about the consequences,' I tell her, hoping that that will see an end to it. It doesn't.

The day doesn't improve as I exit the bedroom and step on dog shit...in bare feet.

SUNDAY APRIL 4th 2010

There's nothing better than having a beautiful woman wake you up with your first coffee of the day, unfortunately

Carolina was off to serve someone else at another table too quickly.

I needed a coffee (or two), I'd spent the evening before having a beer (or two) with my mate Paul and a bloke at the next table who had been in the toilet with a rolled up five euro note just previously. He'd spent the following fifteen minutes using his lighter trying to light the wick on an electric candle...

Easter and a time when we're reminded of two things, chocolate, and Jesus making an unexpected encore on everyone's day off. However, if, and, when, I ever die can whoever is in charge of the reincarnation department do me a favour if you're reading this up there (obviously I'm going up; destined to play a harp on a cloud for eternity...) and just make sure that I don't come back as a dog? It's not the crapping everywhere. I used to go fishing...that's not a problem. No it's the thought of greeting other 'people' by having a sniff...of their backside? It's the main thing that puts me off. I'm a bit reluctant to even shake hands with some of my mates.

I'd been in a bad mood even before the arrival of Kate's text messages and the discovery of the dog's mess because last night we'd paid a visit to the 'authentic' medieval market. They look impressive with everyone dressed up and rubbish on the floor...and although I hate to moan... they're not exactly medieval prices.

Blimey, 'paid a visit' could never be truer. I ordered some grub from an authentically attired trader (although I didn't realise Adidas had been going *that* long); a plate of lamb, some bread and some pork. However, when he came back with the plates, I had expected that the animals we were about to eat would be dead, or at least in a coma... but what he served me up could still have been happily bounding around in a meadow it was so raw. The pork looked like either Pinky or Perky (although I doubt it was the latter) were standing behind the aluminium medieval cookhouse with chunks hacked out of it – it glowed that pink. And the bread was a dry lump of a Mercadona loaf by the look of it. The price for this mini-feast of two plates of meat and some bread? A mere 43€. I couldn't believe it. Nor could the people who had been waiting patiently with me. As he retrieved my food from his Tudor microwave, having blasted it for several minutes, he pointed to where I should take the food and pay – here they had authentically replaced the till with a leather bag (and no receipt…). I took the food, put it down, and carried on walking…all the way to the seafront where we got fed on five courses of the finest Spanish grub around, and still had change from 20€ - for the three of us.

I mean, is it any wonder they went on the crusades? it must have been a whole lot cheaper to eat on the road than stay at home and pop down the market for some dinner - especially when you can get pretty much the same taste and service by licking a cow…

Going back a bit to what I said earlier…I suppose, at the end of the day, if there is someone up there at the Pearly Gates, checking to see if I can come in or not, and they've read the article I did about religion last Christmas, then I've had it, I think.

Having said that…living in a hot place, full of noise, debauchery and the like won't be much different to where I live now. And if it means I haven't got to learn the harp and wear a sheet then I think I'll take the down escalator come the day.

MONDAY APRIL 12th 2010

At last. Some good news, from the UK, comes when my mum calls to say she's got the all clear from the hospital; the treatment worked. Thank fuck for that.

However, the family worries don't stop with my mum getting over the big C, oh no…Mrs Jones is giving me grief now and we're having the same problem with her as we used to have with granddad - she tends to carry on drinking or eating while walking, or looking, away from the bowl. This is fine in itself but as she walks, a fair amount of food or water will fly from her flapping chops and onto the floor – leaving a mess everywhere. Still on the upside, I suppose she doesn't have the stained trousers…

Bank holiday Monday in the UK but I was working at the newspaper office and not much had changed, well not in a way that made life easier – although it did make it challenging… and still no email.

Actually, I came in that morning to find the boss had 'borrowed' the mouse from my computer so I went to the sales office to use one of their computers, and join the sales girls. We were now printing two editions. But we hadn't got any advertising for the new one that was about to go live on the Costa del Sol. None of us had paid a visit to the area to build up contacts and familiarise ourselves with the place we were to be writing the news about – and nobody wanted to buy advertising space in a newspaper that didn't exist yet. But, Nick had come up with a simple solution. He'd simply copy all the adverts out of the local papers that were already publishing in the area. (Oh dear…)

With that done, my colleague Sarah and I were working from a (crap) map of the area to see exactly what was 'local' when it's five hundred miles away we somehow got the paper out.

Desperate for a front page I came up with an article telling readers what our newspaper was all about in an effort to inform new readers and attract advertising. However, Ken decided at the last minute to lead with an article about the problems some boat owners were having in Torrevieja, our local town – a town five hundred miles away from the readers of that edition of a local paper.

Still it got interesting on the Wednesday when the writs began arriving from the other newspapers for stealing their adverts…

7 (NOT) KEEPING UP WITH LUCY…

WEDNESDAY APRIL 28th 2010

I'd woken up tired. Correction – I didn't get any sleep; fiestas. Now I'm all for folk having a good time don't get me wrong, but can't they do it quietly? All the normal rules are forgotten and whole towns can just shut for the duration. And they don't let on if you're ignorant of the fact either – they presume you know. One experience I had was when my motorbike, that I use every day for work, needed a service. I took it to the workshop and happily watched him wheel it inside. I knew from back in the UK that it'd be half a day at most and planned to call back in the following lunchtime. I did. It was shut. For eight sodding days I had to wait for the doors to open once again, and then wait some more while the actually did the service. They just presumed that I knew – presuming also that I wanted a sheltered parking space for my bike…for eight sodding days! Have I mentioned that?

You see the Spanish use the fiestas as an excuse to forget everything else going on in daily life. You don't get the post that was due last week? 'well it is fiestas…' our previous magazine printer constantly let us down by taking more than the four agreed days to print it because of one fiesta or another.

If you live in a different town to where you work you are in luck because not only can you take off the fiesta days for your 'home' town but, of course, the office will be shut when that town has its fiestas too.

But what are the fiestas really, apart from an excuse to buy a plastic guitar from a dodgy looking vendor who gives the impression that he'll come and steal it back later? And at least a week of watching nervous animals standing around with wide eyes and their knees knocking as your local town makes its attempt and rivaling Bush's 'Shock and Awe' tactics.

No, they're much more than that. Fiestas allow Dads to play dress up and be pirates once again, and for families to spend time together while the youngsters of Spain get happily drunk not only on the booze but on the sheer hell of it. They don't get bladdered and then spend the day looking to bash someone – they enjoy themselves. I guess that's what it is all about really and we should congratulate, and envy them. But one thing is for sure, they do suddenly become religious when the fiestas come along.

Can I just add at this point that if there is a God, it's about time I heard someone gorgeous (or relatively attractive, and female, of course) calling out His name during the throes of sex…with me preferably. But it's not happening.

SATURDAY MAY 1st 2010

I'd met with my old school mate, Lucy, who I'd been keeping up with on Facebook, but unfortunately that was about the only place I could keep up with her.

We went to Benidorm and Mitch came along with his mate Zammo to spend the evening with her son. While we would go off and (I thought) find a nice little jazz bar or something, they would explore the bars, and the girls, no doubt. Lucy was still good looking and fun and we kept it 'friendly' at the start. Although I must admit I'd hoped for something to develop later on…maybe?

After seeing the Michael Jackson tribute magician's act (who was white and just went ooh! like Jackson every time a dove shot out of his sleeve – and he had a lot of doves hidden …somewhere) we found a little Spanish bar with a classical guitarist, who was on his break, playing for the evening. When he came back on the whole place was silent; enthralled by the sounds emanating from the acoustic guitar... This guy could play, and Lucy and I sat back and enjoyed the skill of the guitarist as he picked strings unbelievably fast. I say sat back, Lucy was by this time ordering tequilas for us 'so we can really make it authentic'. I didn't have the heart to tell her tequila came from Mexico but I don't think it mattered as she slammed, and licked like a gringo while I had started to see the room spin. Several Spanish tequilas later, I have no idea how many, she took me back to my hotel. To be fair, she took me to my room and tucked me up in bed before asking the boys if they fancied carrying on partying in town. It was four thirty in the morning by now and I was incapable of saying 'romance' let alone producing some, so they went, leaving me to lapse into a tequila-fuelled coma for a few hours at least.

SUNDAY MAY 2nd 2010

The next morning I was feeling a bit worse than dead. I really needed to start considering whewther my diet was healthy too, breakfast today was a coffee, a fag, a Mars bar and another fag. (If you're American and reading this, Fag = Cigarette, thank you.) But with Lucy gone, and Zammo and Mitch looking a bit green in the car, we drove out of Benidorm and back to normality…a nice cup of tea with the dogs on the terrace. And it didn't take long to get the vomit out of the car either.

Having been out-drunk by Lucy the night before I decided to get back in Hunter/Gatherer/Desperate-bloke' mode and it was time for a change of plan and venue, and luck, hopefully.

I headed for Alicante port, noting along the way that they'd either repainted the old flour factory, or there'd been an explosion…?

I ended up at a charming cafe which stands above the water, playing piped classical music and with sophisticated conversation filling the air. Here you pay about the same for a coffee as you would a small terraced house but the setting was nice…and who knows, I thought, this could be the spot to meet Her.

I got off to a good start when a Helena Bonham-Carter look-alike entered the terrace, only to be followed thirty seconds later by her short, ugly, fat boyfriend. Actually he wasn't short, ugly or fat…but he was her boyfriend, so fair game. While they started eating each other's faces I decided I'd take a few 'arty' pictures of the port.

As I did this I noticed a lovely lady sitting on her own and, biting the bullet, I went over and asked if I could take her picture. Deciding that I'm not some sort of pervert she shyly agreed.

I was just getting into it and 'directing' her when I noticed the sun had now gone in and I was now in the shade. On closer inspection (I looked behind me) it turned out to be her husbands. I say husbands because there can't have been one person inside these clothes – he was huge. It took some, if I do say so myself, pretty good oratory gymnastics to eventually persuade him that my intentions were honourable – my only interest was art…

Still the good news was that although I didn't get her phone number I got an email to forward the photos on to, the bad news though, it was his.

Short of putting an ad in the 'desperate and lonely' section of our paper (it hasn't got one yet but I'm the editor…) I'm not sure what else to do. I've tried the websites that promise you love and all I get is women with funny names. 'Twinkle toes' was one who 'winked' at me but looking at her picture the only resemblance to anything celestial would be a Mars bar. 'Sweet Pea' also sent a 'hug' but, again, a look at her picture suggested said hug would be potentially fatal. The only women I seem to attract these days are either on the lonely side of desperate or they're my aunty. Not officially an aunty of course they just remind me of one.

Whether sacrificing my ideals and my morals (yes I have) is worth it in return for someone I could then be happy with I don't know, but the worst thing is I've come to realise that my best chance of meeting someone suitable is to join some sort of club....unfortunately, the WI springs to mind...

But my luck had to change (for the better) sometime and a call from Nicole made me believe that it could well happen, soon. You may remember I mentioned Nicole some time back; she's a Spanish friend, and she's gorgeous. I've asked her out several times for a drink, cinema and meal in fact anything I could think of but until now the answer has always been 'let's see'. Well, in a triumph for perseverance, last night, me and the lovely Nicole were going for a quiet drink, in a snug little bar, together.

I knew I shouldn't be late as I was meeting her at the bar and it'd be rude for her to have to wait alone so I was determined that (for once) I'd be there early.

I was late, and I was worried. I'd left my son alone in the house and the fridge was at his mercy and my effort to appear cool was immediately in shreds (literally) as I rushed into the bar and caught my shirt on the doorknob –ripping it down the seam at the side. I hurried to Nicole, apologising, out of breath and looking like the Incredible Hulk in reverse. She gave me that amazing smile of hers that pretty much says (by my definition anyway) 'come to bed daaaarling...' I must have been forgiven because she grabbed by face and kissed me passionately while I struggled to tuck my shirt in and then sat me down and looked deep into my eyes. She looked fabulous, assisted ably by the blouse that she wore that exposed more cleavage than would reasonably be decent.

And then her phone rang.

Within five minutes, the caller, who I now hated even though I didn't know them, was sat between us bawling her eyes out over her boyfriend who had just run off with someone else. So there I was, halfway through my dream date that had taken so long to arrange, and listening to two women agreeing on what 'bastards' men are. Time to go and with a pained expression Nicole apologised and said we'd do it again someday. I know I keep on about religion but if there is a God, He is starting to take the mickey if you ask me.

Talking of taking the p… the newspaper sacked my mate Pete, the graphic designer this morning, by text. Nice. Apparently sending him a text –letting him know he was sacked -when he was far enough away that he wouldn't come back, was Nick and Ken's cowardly plan. Pete came back.

The doorbell (sounds like 'Avon calling') rang out followed by shouts of 'you yellow (and 'fat' I believe was mentioned) cowardly bastard' (which didn't sound like Avon calling) which saw Ken and Nick making a hasty retreat into our editorial office. Sarah went and calmed Pete down while I watched father and son sweating nervously in the corner.

Drama over and Pete gone, we got on with writing the news…and watching them, watching the door.

The next thing we heard was the lawyers were involved and Nick and Pete were due to be facing each other in court. Little did we know that was just the start of the problems at the 'paper. Still, they were paying me, sort of, and at least it was getting interesting at work, at last.

However, back on our Urb' things were getting odd again. Now, I can understand anyone who is proud of his or her heritage, their culture, their race etc. There's Sir Richard Branson for example, flying high (literally), stacks of cash and a set of teeth to rival Hooter from the Banana Splits – but a prouder Brit you will not find. So much so that he has been, on many occasions, the 'peoples' choice for Prime Minister of the UK.

There are others – the Chinese for example – who will continue their native and cultural traditions while living in a different country to that of their cultural roots. However, every now and again someone crops up in the neighbourhood who likes to be the 'only one' of their kind in the area. Remember Daffyd from Little Britain? Where I live had its very own Daffyd; in fact, it had several hundred, each claiming to be the only one. The 'only one' in this case was a black man, actually lots of black men. All claiming to be the only black man in the area.

I've met, and talked to, so many new people while writing this and you'd be surprised how many of them have asked if I know Darryl (insert: Nigel, Howard, RJ, Chris, Ben etc.) and did I know that he is the only black guy in town?

We live in a small town, a place where if you have not been talked about – you are probably dead. Most go down the 'well I've never seen him!' route or 'oh him? No he doesn't live around here…' is another common line amongst these dark Daffyds.

There are some however, who stand out from the crowd…albeit sometimes by accident…

8 THE DAY THE BRITS GOT ON THE COUNCIL

TUESDAY JUNE 1st 2010

It looked doomed from the start. Setting aside the fact that the two British councilors who were voted in to office following the May elections didn't speak any Spanish and that the head of one of the two parties in power detested the other - to the point of distributing libelous leaflets defaming their character - before the elections. It didn't bode well and to smug gits like me, it was no real surprise when we heard the rumblings of discontent between rival councilors was beginning to simmer nicely. What was surprising (more for the stupidity than the fact that he did it) was when the Deputy Mayor was caught on video 'allegedly' accepting a 5000 euro bribe in a restaurant in Valencia. I use allegedly in its loosest form there as he was heard on the video saying,

'It's good that you give me large bills – less to carry.'

However, this was just the start of what was to be an extraordinary few weeks.

The Deputy Mayor was arrested following publication of the video by La Verdad (a national Spanish newspaper) and his home and office were searched. The town hall, not housing many (if any) friends, immediately suspended him from his duties and distanced itself from him to such an extent that when I went in and asked questions, in my role as a reporter, the reaction was pretty much, 'Manuel who...?'

Anyway, the Deputy wasn't about to go down alone or quietly (or at all, if he could help it) and was determined to enhance his local reputation from 'a bit of a sod' to 'a total tosser' which, fair play to him, he achieved in record time. First he implicated, more or less, the rest of the town hall, including the Mayor, in the corruption scandal that, so far, had only brought up one name – his.

The Spanish have a marvelous system for law; they arrest you first, so that the implied mud firmly sticks, and then ask for a statement, and then let you go – with no charges – only, of course, if you're innocent, but usually by then it's too late.

So that meant that with pretty much the rest of the town hall now banged up and waiting to give a statement, the running of this town (population 20,000) fell into the lap of the next in line – the Brit; who couldn't speak Spanish

Whether people who don't speak the native language should be allowed to be elected into civic positions abroad is another argument for another day but, and this is only my opinion of course, *but what fucking idiot thought it would be okay to have a guy in charge of a whole town when he doesn't speak the lingo?* It's a bit like asking a goldfish to round up sheep...is it not? Anyway, for a short period at least, the Brit had control.

That was until they arrested the chief of police. With him in the cells and several of his colleagues going through his smalls' drawer in his villa, the mayor was released along with the rest of the town hall to resume duties.

Meanwhile the Deputy, now also free, but on bail, was prowling like a wounded bear and began calling press conferences with his 'executive committee' (that consisted of a man that looked like a (very) tired Colonel Sanders and another who chain smoked nervously through the whole proceedings) and who always remained silent. The highlight was when the Deputy produced a 'signed' piece of paper from the two British councilors agreeing to a coalition with him. He'd actually cut their signature from another piece of paper and stuck them onto a new one quite blatantly and waived their 'endorsement' in front of us all - but hey-ho, they were their signatures were they not?

The party in power had had enough and decided to call yet another press conference but one where the whole committee would announce its decision to resign and form a new organisation. The Deputy, not to be outdone, rose from the audience and grabbed the microphone while the majority of attendees shouted him down. The solution came in the shape of Kylie Minogue who appeared on the juke box to drown out the bear that was the Deputy. He went on to issue a couple of death threats to the two Brits and call the odd press conference but life quietened down a little after that.

TUESDAY JUNE 8th 2010 13:25pm

She's back. Or at least her phone is. As I came out of the press conference I looked at my messages and swallowed hard. Kate had left one, and it said it was urgent. That could have meant anything with her but she wanted me to call her and anyway, a bit more time had passed, she'd have calmed down a bit now.

TUESDAY JUNE 8th 2010 13:55pm

I called and in the strangest, politest and unnervingly, calmest voice she had ever used Kate suggested that as I didn't want a relationship with anyone (I had to tell her something...) then we should become 'Shag Buddies' and just meet up now and again to have sex. Now I've no doubt that this is a great arrangement for some people but Kate didn't seem to grasp the idea that I didn't actually fancy her (yes I know I kissed her...). I did what any self-respecting gentleman would do in such a situation, and told her I'd think about it. Really I was just trying to buy some time but she left, chilling me with the words 'well don't take too long...I'm ready for you whenever'. Scary.

I decided to head back to the newspaper office but on the way I went fruit picking (or scrumping as we used to call it) and soon had the motorbike fully loaded, lemons, oranges, pomegranates and grapes, although I did take the sheep back in the end...

I had to write up the report about the latest adventures of the local town hall. The mood was still a bit sombre and the word 'Pete' was unofficially banned I think after the fun the other day. Ken, the retired army major, was still shell-shocked – mind you the toughest thing he faced in his military years was probably dysentery.

Interestingly (told you), a sweepstake had started amongst the sales staff who were still waiting to be paid...again. So was I, but at least the magazine work brought in some money meaning I wasn't in the desperate situation of relying on the newspaper income like the girls. It was at this point, I think, that it dawned on me that not only were the pair of them a couple of knobs, but they were bullies too. Not nice. Fair enough being a knob – there's a lot of it about and many can't help it, like Ken and Nick. But these girls needed the money and these two fat controllers were holding them to some sort of ransom.

The favourite date amongst the girls was the tenth of the month (they were supposed to have got paid on the last day of the previous month) because most of the advertisers would have paid by then. We'll see...

I went home, fed up with the pair of them, and decided that it'd be a good idea to take the dogs out and get some air seeing as Mrs Jones was in the process of doing a sideways shuffle while trying to sneak furtive looks at the Yorkie I was eating (a chocolate bar, not the breed of dog). As I opened the front door, thinking of Kate, I uttered 'Jesus fucking Christ' supposedly to myself. Outside the Jehovah's had turned up again and greeted my unorthodox prayer with a polite, but embarrassed smile.

Today it's the Ark, and the miracle that involved that strangely competent family of sailors who lived miles from any water. My argument and I think it's a fair one is, that it can't have been easy getting two of everything on board can it? But people who follow religion always have an answer don't they? And Bertie's was no different as he explained that He would have taken care of everything when the waters came. It'd be easy to argue about world famine and unnecessary wars and what He was doing about it but Bertie and Wooshter have grown on me a little so I usually politely nod and agree until they depart for a chat with the next 'brother'. I'd always fancied being called that by a cool black 'dude' but I guess I'll have to settle for it coming from someone who looks like they're auditioning for a part on The Little House on the Prairie...

I've mentioned before that when it comes to religion, I think the Spanish can be a tad hypocritical? I know that we all are at times – how often have you prayed to Him, promising to believe if he'll just get you out of a mess, just this once? Or proudly hearing the girlfriend shout 'oh my God!' as you make love…only to discover that she's seen a spider on the ceiling…

But what other country, that professes to be catholic, gets through as many condoms as the Spanish? I'll tell you, none. When it comes to practicing sex (safe or not) the Spanish are up there with the notorious French, and rabbits.

Having said that, the local priest will be revered and spoken to as if he were God himself – until he's gone, and then they can say what they really think. Nearly every shop, business, workplace and toilet has an image of Jesus (or it could be Billy Connolly) plastered to the wall, although none of them are signed so I guess that rules Billy out…

But take a look at their cars and it's no wonder they have the highest accident rate in Europe too. Their windscreens and dashboards are chock-a-block with Jesus merchandising - Nike could do worse than having a word with the Pope about spreading the brand name – from rosaries to enormous crosses (bearing the not too chuffed Jesus) and what look like, but can't be, photos of 'our saviour.' If they can see through that lot while chatting, and looking at, their passenger then good luck to them. Or do they really believe that God will watch over them? If he does, he's not watching too closely is he?

But maybe, when it comes to religion, the Spanish have got it about right. Use it for days off and to celebrate the Virgin birth by getting totally smashed. Commemorate the conquering of a local town but make the commemoration last considerably longer than it probably took anyway and allow kids to walk around with small explosives in their hands.

Just one word of warning, if you are travelling in a car driven by a Spaniard be careful and watch the road for him because with his religious artifacts stuck on the dashboard it's quite possible that the last thing you'll see is someone resembling Billy Connolly as your face smashes you into the dash…and don't have an open coffin as the last thing you (or your family) want is an image of the Big Yin on your forehead…and a 'TOYOTA' impression next to it.

WEDNESDAY JUNE 16th 2010

On the Urb' rumour has it that a UK lottery winner has taken over one of the local bars. The Rumour Mill is now running at full speed at this exciting news in the area. Reports vary but so far we've managed to narrow the win down to somewhere between a scratch card 20 quid and 1.4 million. The place is going to get a total revamp with top quality food being served by a real chef and not someone's Nan. An upstairs nightclub will soon be open and a full size snooker table is to be installed to make it an exclusive bar for discerning clients. I'm a little concerned over whether he's done his homework on this one. Mind you, as dressing up around here means a clean (ish) vest….you never know

Still it'll be nice to have something different on the Urb – somewhere we can go and relax in comfy chairs and away from the bustle and noise of a bar…hang on, news has come in that he's not applied for planning permission yet…never mind, back to fry ups and piss ups then… as I said just another week on the Urb.

Next door, what used to be the busiest bar on the Urb, by a long way, finally closed its doors if only briefly, as the new owners moved in and cleared up. Having been well and truly shafted by their landlord, the previous bar owners had left the place- to put it kindly – needing a bit of a tidy up. As one of the cleaners put it… 'It'll be fine once we get the last t-shirt out of the toilet…'

Opposite the bars, in the bus stop, was the Indian ice cream lady who was dishing out the 99's and choc-ices to kids (and their mums and dads) by the dozen. An (un) healthy queue had formed so I felt pretty safe walking past her, until, to the backing tune of 'Greensleeves' (played through air horns), she called me over, sort of.

'Oi darlin' aintcha gonna say 'ello then?'

I looked at her first and then the queue of people, who were all looking at me anticipating an answer.

'Er, yeah…you just looked a bit busy there' I stumbled.

'Never too busy to talk to you hon,' she said, and then to everyone else, 'I've asked 'im out loads a times an' 'e never comes – do ya darlin'?'

By now everyone was looking at me waiting for a decent answer as to why I hadn't taken this gorgeous (because she was) woman out. Most suspected I was gay, I think, while the rest just looked at me as if I should be.

Promising I would when I had the time I made my exit sharpish…I had an appointment and you don't keep the chief of police waiting. No you don't, not in Spain anyway.

A local police chief owns a large hotel near the office. Nice guy. But he does have a tendency to put his foot in it at times. For example, the other day a rumour was circulating concerning the complex that he owned that was about to be turned into a location for a couple of night clubs.

A few days previously the rumour had reached my ears; people had heard that he was going to get rid of the hotel and build a block of flats on the land. Another rumour was that he had been promoted and was off to Madrid and so, being a journalist I asked if we could meet up and he agreed.

We met at his bar- with me buying the coffee (he is the police chief) - and I asked him about the two rumours and if he knew anything about what was being said in the area. He ignored the question of his promotion and went on to tell me how he planned to build several shops, bars and discos plus an outdoor swimming pool. He went in to great detail and I checked with him often to make sure that I could put it down in print for the locals to read about. 'Of course,' he said each time.

When my magazine was published at the end of the month, I got a call. From the police chief's 'friend'. He asked me to come and meet them both and warned that the chief was not happy. I had no idea why but went to the meeting fairly confident that there had been some mistake.

The only mistake appeared to be that I had listened to the chief previously and printed what he had told me because now, he and his friend were asking why I had printed a pack of lies and demanding that an apology be printed the following month. I couldn't believe it, I'd checked and checked and only printed what he had said I could – which was nearly everything he'd said anyway. He flatly denied it, but I persisted. I persisted right up to the point when he stared me down and then growled 'you really don't want to upset me anymore David…' I agreed and also agreed to print an apology – either that or I could pretty much count on getting stopped on my bike or in the car fairly regularly in the future.

When he'd gone and it was just his friend and I left drinking our coffees I turned to Juan and explained that he really did tell me it was ok to print all that stuff.

'I know' said Juan, 'but what can you do? Just print the apology and life can carry on as normal….for you. Now…we watch football.'

Have you ever watched footy with a Spanish fan…? No well just don't expect them to be impartial…ever.

You see, when it comes to sport, the Spanish have opinions…and a lot of them, especially when it involves football. Ask any Spaniard which team he supports and you will, by and large, get one of two answers Barcelona or Madrid. Pretty much the rest of La Liga doesn't exist as far as the majority of the population is concerned.

The attitude seems to be 'my team's better than yours, so there'. A Madridista will never, ever, praise Barcelona and vice versa and as far as any other team is concerned fans are looked upon with something akin to sympathy. It doesn't matter where you live – geographically you can live next door to the Mestalla Stadium in Valencia and your team will most likely be either of the big two, or maybe Valencia at a push.

I've seen waiters who are rival fans of the biggest two clubs in Spain (and the universe if you're willing to listen to them) almost coming to blows over a match when they discussed it the next day and I've seen more heated arguments in the street over these two sides than any other subject.

It runs a little deeper than football but retains the tribal connection enhanced during the war (the one that nobody mentions) these regions were on opposing sides and the rivalry between those factions – as we've been reminded of recently – was, and still is, intense.

Having said all that the rivalry between fans is much more childish than serious, for example when Ronaldo left Barcelona for Madrid, overnight he became 'past it' and 'on the way down' according to radio phone-ins from his former (Barcelona) fans. When Madrid lined up 'Los Galacticos' in 2006/7 - a collection of the very best players from all over the world – Barcelona fans would go through the team sheet and reel off the problem with each particular star. Conversely, when Barca took the most valued prize in club football – the Champions League title in 2009 – according the Madridistas, they were lucky.

Spanish fans are a passionate lot – mad about their club to the point of obsession – and expats have a lot to learn from them, mainly that although they are crazy about their club and would do anything to support them but they still don't feel it is necessary to kit the whole family out in the home strip whenever they go on holiday…

MONDAY JUNE 28th 2010

Her eating habits leave a little to be desired and as I'm standing at the sink, washing up, I look down. The noise and commotion coming from Mrs Jones' mouth (who is looking up at me and eating) is exactly the same as that of a waste disposal – just more expensive and with bits flying out the sides… In a month where she has gone through more books than my son has in a lifetime, she has also found the time to systematically wander the house and pretty much have a taste of everything, including me.

I descended the stairs into the pit (or Mitch's bedroom – as he likes to call it) and the aroma of fried eggs and something else – unpleasant – hit me. Leroy was sitting on one side of the bed and Mitch on the other. Next to a steaming pile of dog shit.

'Get that turd out of here!' I shouted.

'I was just going anyway,' said an insulted Leroy.

'No, not you, you idiot, the one next to Mitch's feet!'

I looked at Mitch and said 'Mitch you're eating next to a pile of dog crap,' as if he hadn't noticed.

He looked at me exasperated and said, 'I know dad! I'm eating at the moment and as soon as I've finished I'll clear it up.'

'But you're eating…oh, I give up…enjoy your sandwich.'

A groan from somewhere on the floor was followed by one of Marco's hands and then the other exiting a pile of clothes. Marco, Mitch's Dutch friend, was permanently stoned and the politest person I think I've ever met. With one bloodshot eye half open he said good morning in his impeccable English before returning, tortoise like, back into the pile of clothes.

Mrs Jones, who had followed me downstairs, unaware apparently that crapping in bedrooms is frowned upon (by 50% of the household at least) saw Marco's hand vanish and took it as an invite to play. The last thing I heard as I reached the top of the stairs was Marco asking Mrs J if she would 'please get off…'

FRIDAY JULY 2nd 2010

I headed off for breakfast at Juande's in Santa Pola and it's at this point I'd like to make it clear to all speech therapists that the rain in Spain does *not* fall mainly only the plain , not today it didn't – I was soaked.

Drying off, and once Juan had relieved me of a cigarette, smoked it, and only then brought me my drink, I began asking some of the Spanish locals if they had any ideas about what I could write this month in the magazine. When I explained that it was a mag' aimed at expats they began to get a bit more vocal and excited. It seems our hosts wanted to know a bit more about us. Do we really need all that butter on toast? Why do we have our coffee so hot, and weak? Why do our kids sit still and quiet while the Spanish ones run around freely and, it must be said, noisily?

A nice 'Fry-up' was described by one of the group, who'd 'witnessed' one arriving at a table once, quite dramatically (and, I suppose accurately) as, 'as if the whole farmyard had been slaughtered and put on a plate…'

Our beer (or alcohol in general) consumption leaves them dumbfounded (or rubbing their palms if they own a bar) as their tolerance for alcohol generally lies a little lower than ours.

They went on to say that they find it mildly amusing when, after a coffee or two in a bar, we do their jobs for them and take the empty cups to the counter – to save them the job…? They don't see it that way and ask why we do that but then have nurses look after our sick - instead of family taking over to do the caring as they do in Spain? I suppose they've got a point but I wasn't going to start a discussion on the merits of logic and common sense…not in Spain anyway.

As more people entered the café (a couple of families and a doe-eyed young couple) the noise began to increase - to the point where we were now shouting, along with everyone else in the place, to make ourselves heard.

'Why don't they turn the TV off?' I asked Paco, (a local resident of over 50 years) because he was the nearest and had a possible chance of hearing a few of the words bellowed in his ear.

'Because someone might be watching it…' he replied.

I took a good look around the room and everyone was deep in conversation at their table - apart from the four doe-eyes of course who were just gazing at each other - ignoring the 80's pop video that was currently showing.

'But no-one is watching it!' I shouted to Paco above the din.

The look he gave me reminded me of when I was a kid and had just said something stupid,

'But David,' he said, putting his arm on my shoulder, 'someone might come in who wants to watch it – and they can.'

We continued exchanging pleasantries and polite conversation (as much as you can) until the coffees (and subsequent brandies) had gone and the bowls and bowls of free olives had all been consumed, oh and the radio had been added to the TV 'background' noise…

One heated discussion (it sounds as if they are all about to hit each other if you haven't heard a Spanish café 'discussion') was in full swing about cosmetic surgey and Juan (a local policeman) turned around and asked,

'You'd know about it David wouldn't you – you're not normal.'

'Not normal?' I asked, 'I'm not sure what you mean.'

With that he threw his hands in the air and said, 'Homosexual! Gay! How many other ways can I put it?'

With that Carolina, who had been listening in told him off for calling me not normal and kept pointing and saying how rude it was to call me that when 'homosexual' was perfectly suitable.

I tried, and tried to get them to hear me saying, 'but I'm not gay…' but by then they were heavily into the rights and wrongs of calling gay people 'not normal'. And I wonder why I can't get a girlfriend…?

As we left the cafe, an elderly lady fell in front of us - onto her knees (stop the jokes right there…). She'd tripped on the curbstone and landed on her knees, grazing them in the process. Within five minutes, no fewer than 12 people were around her, telling her to stay calm and that help was on the way. I remind you at this point that she had grazed her knees…

Five minutes more and we had two policemen, an ambulance and the same dozen 'helpers.' It was when the second ambulance turned up (with another police escort) that I started smiling. Paco looked at me but said nothing as the lady was loaded onto a stretcher and driven off, with sirens and lights, to be 'checked over' at the medical centre.

I laughed and Paco asked what was so funny, I told him that if that had happened in Britain, the woman would have picked herself up, brushed off any help and carried on her way, saying, 'I've got to get some lard in for tea – see ya love!'

9 THE PAPERWORK AND THE MESS…

FRIDAY JULY 16th 2010

An evening in and, in my role as a single dad, I sometimes have to play the feminine role so now and again (like today) I send Mitch to the supermarket to get a wheelbarrow full of chocolate and a bottle of wine for me to eat while watching CSI…*just* a joke, just.

I was wearing a sarong. Why? My sister had brought me one back from Indonesia and I'd never used it so I'd thought I'd give it a go. Very liberating but the only problem was that every time I tried to step over the dog (or anything) my foot would stop short and I'd end up in a heap.

After Kate I thought it best to steer clear of anyone much younger than me and, by chance, a friend called to say that she had someone she would like me to meet. Single, affluent, educated and good company she said the woman was 'really nice' and that we would be perfect for each other.

And so we met. It was decided by email that we'd meet somewhere neutral (no, not Switzerland) like a cafe bar and with a few butterflies buzzing around my belly I set off.

We'd agreed on three o'clock but by five past there was still only me, a waiter, three goldfish, and a woman knitting, in the bar. I gave it another ten minutes before I leaned over to the waiter and explained that I was supposed to be meeting someone and that if they did show up could you tell them that I waited.

'That's me!' I heard.

I looked around and the nightmare thought that had just shot through my head became a reality – it was the woman knitting. Excitedly she ran over (still holding the needles) and introduced herself as Louise...

'And you must be Dave?'

The temptation to say 'no, I'm Marvin and I'm waiting for my boyfriend Roger' was almost overwhelming but I just nodded resignedly and followed her back to her table.

It turned out she was knitting a scarf for her grandson. Grandson for chrissake! I'm not ready for that yet and I just wanted out. It truly was like spending an afternoon with an aunty; you like each other but in reality you've got nothing in common. And we didn't. From the moment she informed me that if she drunk another cup of tea that she'd be 'up spending a penny all night' - I had to get away...I'm sure I'd be better off with someone who still has full control of all of their bodily functions...

MONDAY JULY 19th 2010

If he hasn't found out yet, he will. And he ain't gonna be happy. Why is it that when you're trying to help someone out – it blows up in your face? I'd arrived at the newspaper office and the 'papers were late from the printers. Ken turned up (sweating like a priest in a playground) desperately trying to unload a stack that he'd collected for the office and nearby shops.

I had my arms full because the previous night I'd been using some of Ken's private collection of back issues of our newspaper to do some research. I put my stack of Ken's classics down and helped him unload. Keen readers were grabbing the latest issue off of us even as we carried them in and it was a good ten minutes before we got the car emptied and Ken waddled off back to his car and drove away to get some more.

I turned to pick up Ken's classics, which I'd left on a nearby table, to find that the pile of some twenty or so newspapers (that were in mint condition and the one remaining hard copy of each edition) had dwindled to two. People had picked them up thinking they were the latest edition and would be sorely disappointed when they got home to discover that what they were reading had actually occurred roughly twelve months previously. However, they would not be as disappointed as Ken if he discovered what had happened. Honesty is always the best policy…so I lied, and told Ken I needed them a little longer, hoping he'd forget about them, or die of old age.

I went inside in an effort to get some work done but Debbie (who I'm convinced could, and probably has, crushed men with her thighs) was hassling me all morning to sign up to another dating site (this one just for the town of Torrevieja) which, considering the suitable women available on the previous one that covered a wider area, would mean I'd probably be dating my mum.

Luckily, in a way, my desk phone didn't stop ringing all morning so I had an excuse. I learnt from one call from a friend in Madrid that it appears the Spanish authorities (bless 'em) have, once again, changed the rules on obtaining our legal documents– specifically the NIE - which is about as simple as filling in an application form to become an astronaut.

I escaped to my refuge; Juande's café, which is the best antidote to stress in the world, to write up the article.

The NIE; Numero Identificacion Extranjero (similar to your National Insurance number if you're from the UK). This is the most important piece of paper on the planet (if you plan on staying in Spain) and the first thing you need to know is that you will need one of these whatever you plan to do in Spain – except die, and even then you probably can't be burnt, buried or used for spares without carrying it to your grave.

When you do go to collect it you will be informed by your fiscal rep' (if you've wisely decided to use one) to make sure that you wake up at about ten minutes after you've gone to bed. (If you've immersed yourself into the Spanish way immediately upon arrival, and are getting home at about six in the morning, then you will need to take a night off). You see, the world of the fiscal rep' (especially where getting an NIE is concerned) exists in the twilight hours, before dawn. Because that is when the queuing begins…

When you do get to the 'office for foreigners', still bleary eyed (and/or drunk) you will be welcomed by several (beady-eyed) east Europeans and many more Africans who are already in position in what resembles a Soviet bread queue from the seventies. They will look at you as if they are hungry foxes and you, who are wondering where the queue begins, or indeed ends, are a disorientated chicken who has wandered out of the pen. (This, by the way, is exactly how you'll feel). Take note of the different type of bedding being used at this point (it doesn't stay around for long) - because they've camped out for the night – cardboard, blankets, sleeping bags and for some reason the Chinese seem to sleep on top of another Chinaman – but it appears to work for them

It's at this point, when you can't leave because the fiscal rep' has parked the car somewhere even she doesn't know how to get back to, that she will tell you about the ticket allocation scheme. It is now that you realise why these people have been queuing all night. Because once the office opens there are only so many tickets issued – whether you've been there all night or not – and if, after spending half of your adulthood waiting for the ticket (this is just the first step in the process by the way), you find that you are number 51 in the queue and Mr Ying and his mattress, Chai Pin, have got numbers 49 and 50, well, bad luck old chap. Come back and give it another go tomorrow…

However, all is not lost, as your fiscal representative (if they have any salt) will have a scheme in place that will assure you of getting the Spanish Social Security equivalent of Willy Wonka's Golden Ticket. This may eliminate the need to leave home and wave goodbye to the kids on a Monday morning and spend the rest of the week trying (and failing) to get an allocated ticket.

More popular nowadays is the Queue Man/Woman. These are people (often friends or colleagues who take turns) that will get in the queue very, very early and wait until the rep' arrives with their clients who will then take over the position (much to the annoyance of the rest of the queue).

Once you've got your NIE (this involves your rep' returning later in the day to collect it) guard it like you would your kids because if you lose it….guess what…? Yep, you get to do it all over again and as I said at the beginning, you can't do, buy, sell, rent or probably steal anything without someone asking for your NIE number.

THURSDAY JULY 22nd 2010

Back in the office and apparently last night a friend had her handbag snatched by a guy she and her boyfriend had been chatting to in a bar during the evening. They'd spent the evening laughing and joking with the guy (who for reasons that will become obvious we shall call 'shit for brains' or SFB) playing guitar and generally having a pleasant time. However, when SFB got up to leave he casually slipped the bag under his coat and headed for the door. Ever alert Zammo saw this and, in words not suitable for a fifteen year old – except in these situations - declared that his mother had been robbed and the offending, and illegitimate, SFB was leaving rather quickly and that they should give chase to the (now apparently copulating) SFB. Zammo shot out of the door, quickly followed by Mitch and the woman's boyfriend, John. It didn't take long for the younger legs of the two lads to catch the thief, and just like when Dixon of Dock Green ruled the streets, they give him a clip round the ear…and a right to the temple followed by a left to the gut, a knee in the groin and finally a slap from John…sending SFB to sleep. If Jack Warner was alive today he'd be kicking the crap out of the Hoodies I'm sure – none of that PC nonsense for Jack - well apart from him being a PC of course… Anyway, back to the story, Mitch called the police while SFB struggled, and eventually freed himself, from underneath John who'd decided that the best form of defence was to hit him again and sit on him. While the local constabulary made their way to the scene SFB freed himself yet again and legged it. He then jumped in his own car and drove past the bar (twice) generously allowing Mitch plenty of time to write down the registration plate. If this wasn't enough information for the police – earlier in the evening he had shown the group his ID, displaying his address and full name…they picked him up later.

It's party season in Spain - or in other words, summer – time to enjoy the weather and welcome visitors and regulars back to our little patch of Spain. However, be warned as at this time of year the cold drinks flow a lot more freely…while the traffic doesn't. And, dear visitor, remember the vest salesman runs out of stock quickly, so get in there sharpish.

It's the season where a 'quiet' drink on the terrace with friends ends in a full-on session and 'that' bottle is pulled out – the one with the unknown dead insect in it that is used as fuel in most other countries. By the time you've had a couple of glasses and devoured a few cold drumsticks - the world becomes a wonderful place and everyone, including the host's dog, is a 'luvverly' person – with a 'heart o' gold'.

You'll know you've had a good time the night before (particularly if you can't remember) when you go to do your bit for the environment at the bottle bank the next morning and you're there for fifteen minutes disposing of the empties. (Somehow it's just not the same without a Party Seven is it?)

After having a small party yesterday I've realised that another sign of a (successful?) eventful evening the night before is when you see someone you do recognise doing something you don't recognise to someone who should know better…enough said on that I think.

So, it's summer and that time of year when we're scrambling around making last minute preparations for the beer fuelled, grilled meat decathlon that is also known as a barbecue. And as grilling something, until it is either crunchy or working its way through the grill to end up in the coals, is the ultimate display of all things a man can do…er…best, your grill should be a reflection of yourself – and excessively manly…like mine

We had a 'barby' at the party and it was a typical bash at our house, in other words someone else did all the cooking, but as the evening had just got into full swing, so did Sod's law with all its might. I realised I didn't have enough booze or chicken wings, or jelly, just as the shops had shut their doors for the night. Then I got the light bulb going off in my head as I remembered the 24 hour shop down the road…but then on arrival, at its shuttered front door, I realised that this is Spain – and the 24 hour shop shuts at eleven…

SATURDAY 25th 2010

Time to get some work done and as I head off I step over the various pieces of litter that have been dumped by my gate once again. That's one thing about Spain…the bloody mess….which means there are load of flies but I may have a solution (to the fly problem at least).

I've just been reliably informed by my mate John, who knows about these things, that there's a shortage of bees. What that means (apparently) is that flowers will not get pollinated as much meaning fewer flowers in the countryside.

It begs the question 'why?' though doesn't it? Can't they be bothered? And if they can't be arsed to fly around a bit and smell flowers all day (which they call 'work') then what are they doing? If they're not making honey, are they making love? Because if not then it needs to get sorted out.

Now that I think about it I haven't seen many this summer; they're not on the beach getting their nectar from discarded drinks bottles, and John's right I haven't seen hardly any while walking the dogs. Perhaps there's a militant bee out there that's persuaded them after millions of years of hard graft that actually, there's no point in making honey – they don't get paid for it. So that's it. The end of the bees as we know it because they can't be bothered any more…we'll have to stick to treacle.

As for the problem of pollinating, we could put little stripy jumpers on flies and teach them to do it…at least then they'd have a use in life. Sorry about all that, I just needed to get it off my chest.

Anyway, back to Spain, and the mess. Firstly, let's get this straight, when I mention 'mess' it doesn't mean I'm going to go on about the Spanish legal system (which is in a mess) or the Spanish bureaucracy (which is also a mess), or local politics (which is in the shit) but what I want to say is what a bloody mess the place is. Litter, rubbish, dead cow you name it, it's there somewhere on the side of a road near you… If you live in luxury, overlooking the surf and the serfs, then you can stop reading now as this will not apply to you. If you own the mountain you live on, you too can put this book down now and go and whip a slave or something. If you're rich and lonely and possibly not long for this planet…call me, I'll be your friend.

But seriously, the place is filthy, which is in direct contrast to the Spanish - who are fastidious about keeping a clean house and still wash down the doorstep and pavements outside of their town houses daily. But get them out of the front door and conveniently, for them, the whole world becomes their bin. Try driving behind one of them on a scooter and you'll get a better idea of what I mean. I've had a whole (full) ashtray emptied out the window of a car in front of me and numerous Big fucking Mac boxes have clattered me and the bike. Watch them with a packet of chewing gum, or a new pack of cigarettes; the wrapper goes on the floor the moment they leave the shop – and that's just the police. They really are as bad as anyone. The good thing is they will get people who have been a bit naughty, and have been sentenced to do community service, to clear it up. The bad thing is that within twenty four hours the litter will start to build up again.

There used to be some bins on the opposite side of the road from my house. For those of you that haven't seen them, these are communal bins, placed somewhere central, for residents to take their household rubbish to…legally they should only do so after nine in the evening (God knows..?). Anyway, they (permanently) moved the bins 50 yards down the road one day but the local Spanish residents, rather than walk the extra fifty yards, continued to place their bin liners on the road, next to where the bins used to be. Within hours rats would be legging it in and out of the bags, with bloody great grins on their faces, spreading the contents over the rest of the road. When I asked one of the Spanish why he left the bags where he did rather than take them down to the bins, his answer was, 'because the bins used to be here.'

Sport isn't safe either. If you go to football match, look out. You see the Spaniards love nothing more than nibbling on bird food (sunflower seeds) during a game and spitting the seed shells onto the floor, or your head if you happen to be on the lower terrace. Quite what the fascination, or indeed the link, is between watching Real Madrid while eating the Latin equivalent of 'Trill' is I'm not sure. But go to any ground and you'll see a pile six inches deep (I'm not kidding) of shells that have been spat out over the years. They just use the help of gravity and sweep them to the lowest point in the terrace, and leave them.

And while I'm at it… the next time you're in a Spanish town head to the smartest restaurant and go in the Gents toilet. This will consist of a broken seat, no toilet paper, a bin full of used toilet paper and a toilet full of what the last visitor had for lunch. It always amazes me that they seem to forget about this room but then the Spanish treat anything out of the house as something they can make a mess of; including nature – if it's got fur, eat it. Go in any Spanish home and it will be immaculate, they just seem to consider everywhere else, and everything else, fair game.

FRIDAY JULY 30th 2010

After discovering another sink-full of dirty dishes I'm beginning to believe that living with a teenager is reason God invented wine; without a glass (or three) in the evening parents wouldn't survive. It should be on prescription in my opinion.

Mitch has a taste for fried egg sandwiches. Which is great, he's a growing lad and eggs are full of protein and…well stuff that's good for a six foot six inch teenager, I would have thought. The trouble is he never, ever washes the frying pan. His reason? According to Mitch there is no point as 'I'm only going to use it again tomorrow…' my argument to try and make him see sense was that he could apply that rule to everything and end up washing nothing was met with a sigh and a rolling of his eyes that clearly meant I'd just got the point, 'yes, I know!' he said. I give up.

Jane has emailed me about our meal out the other night. I'd made the 100 kilometre trip down to see her near La Manga and had a night to remember that was for sure. To be honest I'd been diving nearby during the day with Mitch and some friends and while he'd headed back with them, Jane and I had agreed to meet up for a meal.

Although she talked a lot, when she did stop, she became quite attractive. When we'd emailed each other before meeting up she'd told me about how she was 'internationally travelled' which she may well have been - but she still sounded like a Wigan lass when she talked, and, oh boy, could she. The other thing she forgot to tell me about was her worry or paranoia as it's often called. You see while she was 'internationally travelling' she got internationally up the duff by an Arab. And now she was convinced that he was coming back at any moment to snatch the child – after 12 years. I must admit it was a little less than romantic when she also mentioned that she'd spoken to all the police locally and they would be watching me as I arrived at her house.

The intrigue continued all evening too as in between mouthfuls of curry at an Indian restaurant she filled me in on all the different ways 'he' could get her child out of the country and of her plans to dodge him, it was at the curry house that things had taken a slightly sharper turn for the worse.

The Indian restaurant was in an industrial unit, on an industrial estate and it was empty. Apart from a half-hearted attempt to make the place look authentic we were basically eating in a warehouse. One that was rich in tables but on the breadline when it came to that niche of customers in search of a curry delivered by fork lift.

After half an hour or so the wine was starting to have an effect on Jane and the conversation was turning to the sleeping arrangements and if, when we went to bed later, it would be in the same house. I put my hand on hers and looked into her eyes and nearly threw her under the table when an incredible noise shook the room. It came from the kitchen. To give her credit, she held on well. Then the kitchen door opened and out came four chefs dressed in traditional Indian attire dancing to the extremely loud and horrendous racket. Jane, who'd presumed that this was the start of some snatch attempt, was frantically calling the baby sitter on speed-dial while I shoved my fingers in my ears. Why she was calling home when the commotion was quite clearly (and audibly) here I couldn't work out and it was so loud that there was no way of holding a conversation so I had to sit there and smile politely at the dancing chefs until they had finished…more than ten minutes later.

Panic over and the local SWAT team stood down we carried on with the meal and again things were looking pretty good, I hadn't even spilt anything yet, but, twenty minutes after the first 'ambush', the second wave came from the kitchen. The chefs were at it again and we had to sit through another ten minutes (of the same dance and music) until they'd returned to the kitchen.

Four times that happened in two hours and by the end of it I couldn't wait to get on my motorbike and drive the 100 kilometres home, alone. Ah well...at least I'd get to see Match of the Day.

Twice! Bloody twice I got stopped on the way home – by the Guardia – and so did my only other chance of using the word 'score' in this chapter, I'd missed Match of the Day. What was I stopped for? For not stopping completely still at a 'Stop' sign on a straight country road at eleven at night. A junction that allowed me to see so far, in each direction along the road that I was joining, that I swear I could see French people riding bikes with onions around their necks.

'Have you read your Spanish highway code?' asked the second Guardia team to stop me. The first had merely stopped me for a roadside check and had sent me on my way with a grunt after looking at the papers for my motorbike.

'Of course I have!' I lied.

'Then you know you should stop at the junction - not pull out without stopping.' He said with a little dance and a flick of his truncheon before spinning round like Michael Jackson (not really, that just conjured up a good image...), 'it is a very serious offence to do this; two hundred euro fine...' he added.

I pleaded with him; stating my case that I was a safe driver, (had a few crashes...) and always obeyed the rules of the road (3 speeding fines this year, so far) and finally I got down on my knees (ok...another fib), but I did plead with him and point out that it was possible to see our garlic-munching cousins, the road was so long, and clear.

'I know', he said. And he and his mate both laughed 'have a good night'.

'Bye, bye' he said in English as I drove off....

'Tossers' I thought as I smiled at him.

So if you live in Spain or are thinking of moving over set aside a few years and read the Spanish Highway Code, or the Koran – which is a shorter version.

To top off what had been a rotten evening, I got home to find Mrs Jones happily chewing on the TV cable, so that was that for watching anything. All that left me was the internet so I visited a few expat forums and found one which had a request for any information on obtaining a Spanish Highway Code where someone had replied, 'I didn't think anyone knew enough about driving in Spain to write a highway code....'

10 OF COURSE I'VE READ IT…

The Spanish Highway Code is reputed to be the most comprehensive in Europe, which means to you and me that it is really long. No surprises there as we know our hosts are partial to using the odd forest or two for official paperwork. For example we had a letter from a guy who had to take an exam for a fishing licence (eh?) and having anticipated a multi-choice 25 questions or so, this little beauty ran through one hundred pages of legislation.

Of course, our Spanish cousins are not daft, this has the benefit of creating a massive industry made up of, interpreters, gestores, and lawyers etc., who will, for a fee, hold our hand and guide us safely through the labyrinth that is the Spanish admin maze and it doesn't hurt the booming paper industry either.

Sections of the Spanish Highway Code, besides containing actual codes that would be useful for, er, say, driving, and informing the (by now comatose) reader of the rules of the road (oh yes there is…), also cover such items as first-aid, vehicle maintenance and even the loads (and types of loads) carried by vehicles.

A warning for rule-breakers comes in a polite (but clearly ominous) threat which says, 'The Spanish Traffic Police are considered efficient in applying their laws and it is highly recommended that if stopped, friendly cooperation with their requests should be applied...' uh huh. Unlike the British Bobbies, the Guardia won't take a mouthful of abuse and politely nod, still calling you 'sir until you have finished, and then wave you on your way. The only people who tend to get away with it are the elderly who (still) command such respect in this country. I once watched an old fella, who looked so old I think he may have been clinically dead, calling two Guardia Civil officers every possible Spanish insult...and then he started on their mothers. He still got away with it. But, as stated above the official advice is not to...

But now you're driving in Spain (please use your imagination if you're sitting in a flat on a rainy day...in Slough), and, of course, you've read your highway code (or like the rest of us, assumed that it's pretty much the same as the one back home, and got on with it...)

Have you remembered everything? The keys, fags/chewing gum (optional), your phone, sat nav, kids (again optional), and maybe a map? Good, so now you're ready, well almost, because, on the road in Spain, on top of that little list the driver must also carry proof of their identity, a driving licence, valid insurance, the vehicle registration, the receipt for the insurance, proof of a current ITV (MOT), a spare pair of specs (only if you have been prescribed them – obviously...) and a Goldfish (just seeing if you were still paying attention).

Then there is the little matter of what else should be in the car, ready? Ok, deep breath... Spanish law requires that every vehicle carries two Red Warning Triangles, a First Aid Kit, a Fire Extinguisher, two high visibility jackets and a set of spare bulbs.

So that little run-around needs to be gotten rid of and an ex-Securicor van bought so you can carry all this stuff.

But be warned because if you should decide that - for some really important reason - you need to break the speed limit, the Guardia, if they catch you, will quite happily give you a fine based on the speed you were flying along at to get home and save the cat from starving. The latest info I have is that it is 6€ for every kilometre over the limit. Other offences are calculated, more or less, at the discretion of the officer present. (See what I said earlier…be nice…)

The other thing to remember is that if you have a foreign registered car and are doing something illegal – such as parking on a yellow curb etc. you will get towed. A foreign car, illegally parked, is not a good idea. In fact, slapping an officer on the backside, with a banjo, may be less problematic or obvious. And, if you've got a rent a car, don't think that you'll blend in like the natives just because you've pulled the sticker off. Rental cars are as easy to spot and common as white stilettos in Essex and will enjoy the same treatment as a foreign car. The reason? Because you have put your name and passport details to so much paperwork the authorities know that, one way or another, they will get the fines paid.

The rent a car industry in Spain has learnt an awful lot from a certain Irish airline operator. Imagine that you've just had a two hour flight listening to some Lithuanian trying to sell you aftershave and spent two hours previously in the departure zone of an airport back home (which was more expensive than Monaco) and endured the last thirty minutes watching everyone else's luggage passing on the carousel before yours finally appeared. Now you just want to get to your intended destination as quickly as possible. The only thing standing (sitting actually) in your way is Felipe from Belgium, the clerk at the car hire desk, who boasts the charisma of a slug…but works a little slower.

Frustrating isn't it? And by the time they've finished adding up all the 'extras', on top of what seemed a good deal when you booked it on the internet, you feel like you've been financially abused by Felipe, if there is such a thing, if not I've just invented it. Don't get me wrong, I'm not knocking all of the guys and girls in the rent a car offices – I used to work with them and some of them are kind and helpful but the Felipe's of this world exist...so we'll pick on them.

You see over the years things have changed in the car hire world especially here in Spain, less than ten years ago travellers were happy with a Seat Marbella (Fiat Panda) that had no aircon, no power steering, no stereo, no airbags or even comfort come to that. But with the advent of the internet based companies over recent years, who have offered more and more for less and less in an effort to beat the competition, customers now require all the luxuries but at the super-low prices that, on first impression, look very accommodating indeed. But...what you see, or more accurately, what you expect, is not quite what you get.

Somehow or other 'Autojumbo' (our fictional car hire company for this exercise so I don't get the shirt sued off my back...) can squeeze 50€ euros worth of fuel, that you must pay for, into the car that you've rented which is roughly the size of a wheelie-bin. Whether they are using aviation fuel or not I'm not sure. Another charge is a baby-seat which if you plan to spend more than a couple of weeks here means that you might as well have left the little darling at home – with a full time nanny. I've not even started on the 'extra drivers' tick box yet but I know, from experience in the industry and (because in Spain the car is insured not the driver) that it costs the hire company no more money to add drivers...but they charge for it handsomely.

But you knew all this already of course...because you read the terms and conditions on the website? Just watch out for that one because on several sites I couldn't even find any. On those that I did they were about as vague as a Spaniard giving directions. They also cover themselves (but unfortunately not you) by telling you which bits of the car aren't included in the insurance that comes with the car. For example, tyre damage, damage to the underneath, flat battery, days off road after you've hit a pothole… it goes on, and on. However, those kind people at Autojumbo will offer you an insurance (at an extra cost) that will cover the bits that aren't covered…still with me? good because in the small print of *that* insurance you'll find Mr Vague has been busy again and inserted the line 'exclusions from insurance can be partially covered with this insurance…' of which there is no explanation as to exactly what it is you are covering, or not.

So you end up paying a load of 'extras' that Felipe has now convinced you it is not worth hitting the streets without, even though you haven't got a baby, and off you head feeling like you've just paid for enough fuel to get the plane back to the UK again.

Why all the extras? Because with the emergence of the online and what seem at first glance, 'budget' companies the price to actually rent the car is extremely cheap, so they need to make it up somewhere, and Felipe is not letting you out of the car park without relieving you of a good few swipes of the credit card first.

My advice, if you come over, is stick with the small guys – the price you see is the price you get, and the service will be so much better. Find a reputable company and deal with the owners (usually) directly and you'll get straightforward answers…no small print, and no Belgian tossers. Time for bed after all that I think.

WEDNESDAY AUGUST 11th 2010

An early morning call from the Jehovah's witnesses, Bertie and Wooshter. I'd heard them coming before they rang the bell; their sandals were slapping on the tarmac like a slow double hand clap, so I was ready for them. Even though I had woken up about every twenty minutes during the night expecting a load of grinning Indians to come dancing into the room I was in a fairly good mood, and vowed not to swear in front of B and W.

But it wasn't Bertie or Wooshter when I opened the door. The Gestapo were standing in front of me. To be accurate one of them looked like Herr Flick from 'Allo 'Allo….and so did the other. Bertie and Wooshter were obviously busy elsewhere and they'd sent the SS in their place.

'Gut morning…er…' he said pausing and looking at a piece of card in his hand that was clearly a list of people to visit (victims…?), '…David!' he shouted, eventually. 'Ve have come to talk to you about ze joy of God (which sounded like 'goat' or perhaps he did mean goat – there are some strange people about you know).

'My goat is your goat – you understand David?'

'Yup', I replied.

'Zer ees only vun goat for all of us and He ees viz us all ze time…especially ven ve are on our knees; our goat ees right zer in front of us, answering our prayers and fulfilling our dreamz…you understand David?'

I thought that it was probably against the law, but answered yes, I understood.

'Ve shall kneel now and become von viz goat?' said one of the Flicks.

I declined, politely, said I had to give the lads a lift and better be going, managing to shut the door before anymore farmyard animals were introduced.

I quickly checked my emails before I left and saw there was one from Kate, with an attachment simply titled 'us'. Oh shit.

I opened it and to be honest it was the nastiest thing anyone had written about me (that I'd seen). Well apart from Mr Sandhurst's report at school but he never liked me, and I only let his tyres down once…(every week…for five years). Shaking off the memory of school (oh crikey…Carolyn, where are you now…?) I got back to Kate's letter. To put it in a nutshell, she hoped that my business went bust, I got ill and that no woman would ever have to suffer by being in a relationship with an 'ageing bastard like you'.

I think it's over….

WEDNESDAY AUGUST 18th 2010

Off to Rugby with my lad, Mitch, and his mate, same old story…one of the Mums said weeks ago that she'd be willing to take the boys if I could pick them up. No problem. However, I've been taking and dropping them off every week since…I don't mind really – you do get used to it as life on the Urb breeds not only complacency - as we gradually fall in line with the Spanish way of putting things off – but also downright laziness in some. The Spanish have got it right; they'll just promise the earth and forget to deliver but at least you know where you stand with them. One silver lining to this little drizzle cloud was what we found on the journey there: a local Spanish farmer riding along the road on his ancient push bike with a rocket launcher strapped to the crossbar – including rocket. And biting on a very dead and very raw fish (including head and fins), I nearly had to look twice, I mean, come on, fish on a Wednesday…?

But seeing the cyclist precariously, and hopefully, making his way home got me thinking again about the way the Spanish drive, I mean it's no bloody wonder they hug each other whenever they arrive is it…?

I reckon that the last thing the typical Spanish rabbit hears - before it becomes seriously vertically challenged and is spread over the tarmac - is not, as in the case of the British rabbit, the squeal of tyres as they skid and swerve, trying to avoid the imminent collision. No your typical Spanish bunny hears the continuous hum of a well-oiled (and fast) engine as the driver of the car doesn't contemplate releasing pressure on the accelerator and avoiding Fluffy.

For some reason the most laid back and unrushed nation in the world become Joey Barton with attitude as soon as they get behind the wheel, but why? Nobody seems to be able to answer that one but for all our similarities as western Europeans, there are some serious issues out there that our hosts could do with looking at…if only for the Fluffys of this world…

Have you ever been in car with a Spanish driver? It's no wonder they've all got Rosary beads in them - it'll save time later on. Inches from the rear bumper of the car in front, they will have a different (read: homicidal) logic. Ask, what you think, is a sensible question, such as,

'Hey Jose, what are you going to do if the car in front should brake while we're trying to read his dashboard clock?'

He'll reply with, and this is the same for all Spanish drivers I promise you, 'why should he brake – we're on a main road with no turn offs for a long time, mi amigo.'

'But what if a rabbit should….oh yes, sorry, forgot.'

If they are going to turn left, beware, because although the indicator may be signaling to you that he intends to turn left - he may well be going right. Although if he is going left, still beware, because he will need to swing the car right before making the left turn, totally confusing you. However, no indicator at all does not mean that he is not going to turn off – he may well suddenly hit the brakes (not for Fluffy) and swing into a turning - causing chaos behind him, but that's behind him, and therefore does not exist…

If your driving speed is not approaching the sound barrier while on a main road then expect a Jose to sit on your bumper – with the occasional blast on the horn to move you along a bit – and then watch as he pulls out of your slipstream and passes the line of cars that you've been following for the last five miles, until it comes down to a game of chicken between him and the car coming the other way.

Parking comes across as just a big game of pinball to the Spanish driver, I think. Picture the parallel parking that you've done all your life back home; fairly slow and gentle as you move in to the parking spot, being careful not to touch the cars at either end. Now imagine putting a Kangaroo in a Volvo that's got an iffy clutch and you have the Spanish driver trying to park.

However, the Spanish driver does have one redeeming feature. If they should notice something and you haven't, they will flash their lights, blast the horn, overtake while waving their arms and shouting furiously and then swerve in front and screech to a halt - blocking the road and drawing the whole world's attention on you - to tell you that you've left your lights on…

11 WHEN A MELON JUST ISN'T ENOUGH…

SATURDAY AUGUST 28th 2010

I've just got back from the airport. (where'd I'd spent ten minutes trying to work out what a banner across the road that spelt 'ATOV' meant in Spanish. It finally dawned on me that it was an election appeal, and I was looking at it from the back…)

Anyway they've gone. You pull away from the airport, blow a big sigh of relief and think about watching telly tonight, in peace. You also remember, with a smile, that you can have your bed back and won't have to make tea in the morning for, what felt like, half a platoon of brightly coloured soldiers. Actually, that's not the best analogy in the world…soldiers by job description have to be tidy and organised, but you get my drift?

The relatives, 'friends' and the downright hopeless have been over to stay, spending half the time of their two week 'visit' (seems like months) telling you how horrible the UK is and how well you're looking.

When they are in the queue at the checkout and for some incredible reason that defies logic; the checkout girl has taken the liberty of speaking to them in Spanish, they'll have looked at you without saying a word, expecting you to translate, which you do by reading the amount on the digital display in front of them what they can clearly see for themselves..

They will have said that they are coming to 'visit you' but we know that what they really mean is '*it's holiday time!*' and by the time you've shown them to their (your) bedroom and they've had a rest from travelling (because sitting on a plane for two hours is apparently 'exhausting') they are ready to head out for a drink, and something to eat. Despite the fact that just yesterday you filled the freezer, the cupboards and the fridge with enough food to keep the Falkland Islanders going through a dodgy winter.

'no....you shouldn't have to cook for all of us' (not tonight anyway) 'let's go out and get something and you can relax and have a drink' (one that you'll need as you face a night on a sunbed, in the spare room).

Once you've paid for the drinks, everyone heads home to start on the fridge's stock of alcohol and your favourite bottles of wine while you head up to bed, knowing that you've got to get up in the morning. And on it goes for the next two weeks or so. Or is that just me?

Just recently a friend has returned home to the UK following a two week 'visit' and I'm not exaggerating when I say that a quadriplegic would have been more helpful around the house than him. He did a bit of shopping, I must admit, when we ran out of fruit he bought a melon...which he ate. And some white wine...which he drank. It begs the question as to why people suddenly think that your home is a hotel and you, unfortunately, are the maid, chef and manager. I mean, can you imagine going to stay at their house, during the week, when they have to get up for work every day and insisting that they come and eat out nearly every night after you've been cloud-bathing all day?

However, I have a simple answer my friends, one that will benefit all and allow you to get on with your life while they're over for a holiday...I mean visit. Get them to rent somewhere. Tell them you're full those weeks, got cockroaches or perhaps a regional disease and then offer them the services of the many reputable rental companies that offer properties at that time of year. They could rent a car too (saves you driving them around) and the local supermarkets would benefit from their frequent trips to top up on water as they'd 'rather not' drink from the tap.

That should solve it and when they do go home after their trip you will not be knackered from having spent the last two weeks picking up wet towels, dirty ashtrays and anything else that happens to be left lying around and they'll have helped the Spanish economy, everone's a winner?

Ah well…I've got my house back, time to relax.

SUNDAY AUGUST 29th 2010

'Better get your wallet out dad', said Mitch as I sipped a lovely glass of red on the roof terrace while enjoying a decent book.

I laughed, 'don't think so sunshine…you had money yesterday, and anyway, what for?'

'Ice-cream, you know it's better for you if you cough-up the cash now dad, or the ice cream lady will want to know if you're in or not…?' he smiled.

'Right, well seeing as said ice cream lady isn't about at the moment (no bloody 'Greensleeves' had been heard) – I don't need to give you anything…so sod off!'

You have to stamp down hard on these kind of threats you know, or before you know it…well, they'll have you eating out of their hand.

He told me that she was in fact parked at the bottom of the steps to our apartment and preparing an assault on the door as we spoke.

'Her thing that plays the tune is broken',

(Apparently a disgruntled punter had shoved his 'Funny Feet' ice cream into the speaker and 'Greensleeves' was silenced - he should have got a medal.

Ten minutes, and eight euros, later she was gone and normal service was resumed on the terrace; a nice Rioja, a good book, some light jazz…and Mrs Jones churning one out that would have made Nelly the elephant's eyes water…

MONDAY SEPTEMBER 8th 2010

An interesting journey into work today mainly because I was stuck behind (what looked like) a Buddha wearing Lycra…but what turned out to be just another pain-in-the-arse cyclist.

The brightly coloured gits appear as soon as the weather warms up to ruin your journey. They swarm around you with their glassy eyes looking, no leering, at you, and act as if they own the bloody earth not just the road. The more of them there are, the more annoying they are. No sooner has the temperature risen above what equates to 'bloody freezing' out here and you'll find them. Blocking the road.

It wouldn't be so bad if they came out in ones or twos, but no…this is Spain they need to cycle around the one lane country roads in groups like Chinese commuters. And then, not satisfied with blocking the road and forcing you to go so slow that your cigarette smoke overtakes you, they'll have a little chat amongst themselves. Blowing the horn doesn't work (I watched an ambulance struggling to get past a group of cyclists one day) and running them over just means a lot of paperwork. So instead of driving through the countryside and admiring the far reaching views you end up staring at Jose's (the fat accountant) sweaty backside for hour after hour.

That wouldn't be so bad if they didn't feel the need to wear 'all the gear.' While Lance Armstrong might look good belting along the French roads; his toned muscles glistening with sweat as he pedals faster than my mum has ever driven, Jose, the chunky bean counter, does not. Obviously Lycra is meant to aid aerodynamics and that is fine on old Lance but if he had to ride around with the equivalent weight of Kylie Minogue stuffed up his shirt all the aerodynamics technology in the world is not going to help. Put a Hippo in Lycra and sit him on your chopper (that's a bike) and see how gracefully he cuts through the air, not.

The mountain bikers are not much better either. It doesn't matter if you're out for a quiet walk or standing chatting – they have got to go through without the inconvenience of having to turn their handlebars and at about 1000 miles per hour. If you watch they'll even try and impress you with a little jump here and there – even Jose's brother will be there – before pedaling like fury in the direction of the next rambler. One chap made the mistake of playing 'Dare' with Mrs Jones once – he lost…

A worldwide ban on cycling or just wherever I go will do. Perhaps we could have stickers on our cars that would warn the cyclists if we are 'cycle friendly' or not, in which case any car sporting a sticker showing a cyclist with a tyre mark running through him would be best avoided by the cyclists. But that won't work because like your average Spanish driver they never, ever look behind them. Ever.

The highway code doesn't help either giving them all sorts of 'rights' even though they pay nothing to use the road and stating that they have right of way over a car '*When a motor vehicle turns right or left to enter another road, and a cyclist is near he has priority…*' huh? No, I'm sorry cyclists but it's time to ban it, it's dangerous for a start and riddled with drugs (just look at the Tour de France every year and you'll see more needles than a WI knitting club). If you break down, i.e. get a puncture, you have to push and the clincher as far as I'm concerned is surely you have to question any sport that requires a man to shave his legs…

Just one more thing for any cyclist reading this, yes mate, compared to you I do own the bloody road.

MONDAY SEPTEMBER 13th 2010

At work I'd been designated the job of researching Saffron for a feature in the next issue so I went on the internet and began my search and discovered a couple of things… firstly Saffron is the most expensive spice in the world (it can cost up to 250€ per ounce) and, secondly, Saffron is also a high class call girl from Minnesota who presumably doesn't charge by the ounce…although if she did, being American, that would probably make her very expensive.

But apparently our readers will be more interested in the spice (Minnesota Saffron also offered 'spice' by the way) so I'd better stick to those pages. At last it's quietened down a bit round here though, for a while at least.

FRIDAY SEPTEMBER 17th 2010

Another row at the office and this time it's Donna the sales manager, which seems a bit strange as she was shagging the man she was arguing with just a few weeks ago on a 'sales trip' to Madrid, - Nick, the boss.

Apparently tough taff Donna had stormed into his office demanding that the girls be paid only to be told, once Nick had put his Big Mac down, to fuck off. Not very romantic, but then neither is a bunk-up with a sweaty bloke in a cheap hotel in Madrid…I'm told. So that left Donna stomping, and muttering, her way around the office - sounding like she was saying her Rosary - while the rest of the girls were either crying or not being very complementary about our glorious leader. Although I had to argue one point in his defence. Being a bloke, I know, it's impossible to be both tight-fisted and a wanker at the same time…having said that – he gave it a bloody good go.

It's a lot quieter and back on the Urb and the Madri…Madrilene…Madrilinio... (The people from Madrid) have gone back to their lives in the capital – until Easter at least – and we get our parking spaces back. The relatives, mostly, from the UK, have gone and things have calmed down immensely.

Calmed down that is unless of course you are a Spanish bus driver… have you ever got stuck behind a bus in Spain? Thought not. It's impossible because they drive so fast that the vinyl lettering peels off the side of the bus and rabbits in nearby fields are swept from their feet by the passing gust. Whether their time-tables are so finite that they need to get their foot down or they just like going fast I don't know – but I wouldn't mind betting that they have a 'lap record' chart on the wall of the bus garage.

I met a tramp this month (not that sort, this one was free, sort of) walking the road with his trolley full of possessions and the two obligatory scruffy looking dogs following in his squeaky wheeled wake. He sat next to me on a bench and asked (politely) for a cigarette and we began chatting. I asked him where he was going, as he puffed away and he looked at me (through fairly glazed eyes and a 'Bellamy beard') and looked down the road which he had been heading and said 'that way'.

Ok…

'So where have you been?' I inquired.

He looked at me again, looked in the opposite direction and said, 'that way'.

Not put off I asked what he was going to do for the rest of the day but that just about merited a shrug before he shut his eyes and went to sleep.

I got up, left him the rest of my cigarettes and began walking away…only to hear him utter (with his eyes still shut), 'you worry too much young man, enjoy today and tomorrow will still be there.'

Yeah…it will won't it.

I headed for Juande's Café where at least the atmosphere was peaceful…if not quiet.

I know I've written about Juan before. But suffice to say that he never ceases to amaze and amuse not just me, but everyone who becomes a 'victim' of his unique brand of table service in a Spanish cafeteria. It's not unusual for Juan to help himself to a patron's cigarettes, if said patron has been daft (or generous) enough to leave them on the table in front of them. However, in his defence, Juan sells the best donuts in the world and at the weekends I usually grab a couple to have with my coffee.

On Saturday he excelled himself once again by, amongst other things, forgetting our order and telling a customer that if she brought her dog in the café...his would probably abuse it.

He is lately also insisting on speaking English because of the amount of foreign visitors around but this is his English which consists of him saying, 'Haalo...how are you?'

And when asked the same question back, his response would be,

'I am super fandango'

Which in Juan's world is English...because he heard it in a film once.

Pleasantries and fandangos out of the way we ordered our toast (I'd decided against the donuts for a change – a big mistake as it turned out) and coffee from Juan who promptly disappeared, although not to get our order but to chat to a friend who had just come in. Soon the friend was laughing loudly at Juan's banter and after what must have been a good ten minutes he moved on to a table of housewives with whom he, once again, began joking and laughing.

After about thirty minutes we were starting to get hungry and Lolis, his long suffering wife, must have noticed as she asked us if we wanted anything today. Isn't it great the way the Spanish will ask you that? While you're sat in *their* café? And it doesn't matter if you say 'no, I just wanted to sit down a while' - they won't bat an eyelid. Anyway, we said yes, we'd ordered from Juan already. Cue the row. Lolis shouted at Juan across the café that we had been sitting there for a long time and where was the order? Juan's shrug said it all and he came back over smiling and laughing, asking what we wanted, again. This time he managed to cross the six feet of floor to the bar and order our breakfasts without interruption. It was a few minutes later that Lolis (always on the ball) realised that Juan was still in the restaurant and hadn't gone to fetch the fresh donuts (that I hadn't ordered) from the nearby baker. Not happy with seeing her husband slacking (again) she told him to get moving or my coffee would arrive and I wouldn't have my donuts. Holding his hands up defensively, Juan explained that I didn't want donuts today and that I'd ordered toast but that wasn't good enough for Lolis who told him not to be stupid and stated that, 'David always has donuts at the weekend…'

To his credit, Juan held his ground with her for a good five seconds before walking off shaking his head towards the bakers. I stopped him outside and asked where he was going. He told me he was off to get the donuts,

'But I don't want them Juan' I insisted.

He just looked over my shoulder at his wife, back at me, shook his head…and trudged off towards the bakers.

Nothing is quite as simple as you think in Spain is it? I decided I'd go back in and make it all better between Juan and his wife and explain that I didn't want the donuts this week and that it wasn't Juan's fault.

Lolis, being a Spanish housewife, explained to me why I wanted the donuts and ended up by informing me that, in a nutshell, that I should eat them.

'you don't eat…you die…now eat!'

I ate.

12 GETTING FRIENDLY WITH THE LOCALS…

FRIDAY SEPTEMBER 24th 2010

It was around this time, and following my event-filled night out with Jane, that I decided that finding a woman wasn't quite as simple as it was when we were teenagers. Back then you asked them out, they said 'yes' or 'no' and you walked off either way. Now, I find I'me walking on eggshells just in case I end up offending someone or they get the wrong idea…like Sharon. Or it could be just me…

Sharon was the single mum of one of my son's ex-girlfriends and a very nice person too, and she liked a drink. When I say she liked, I mean she loved it, and she'd keep going until her eyes glazed over and she was poured into a taxi and sent home. She called me one night when Mitch was at her house and asked if she could come round, I think that's what she said as she was slurring quite a bit at the time. I made up an excuse that I was just on the way out with friends and she, generously, offered to come along. I couldn't face having to carry her to a taxi later on– truth was I couldn't have carried her without the aid of a Chinook anyway and I didn't fancy fighting off her hands all evening, which is what happened last time. I called a couple of mates and told them we had to go out as I had an idea that Sharon could well turn up at my house. I needn't have worried. She was in the first bar we walked in to.

Everyone said hello, although she seemed to be lining me up for last, and when I stepped forward I went to give her the traditional peck on either cheek, she grabbed my testicles, firmly. And held on to them. She refused to let go until I could provide her with an acceptable reason why she shouldn't come back to my place. The fact that she was sweating, drunk and at present the custodian of my genitals were reason enough and perfectly acceptable to me, but not her apparently.

Although her eyes couldn't actually focus anymore her grip remained firm for a further few minutes until I managed persuade her to let me buy her another drink. That done, I left and headed home looking like I'd just ridden a shire horse for a week.

As I lay in bed, throbbing, I couldn't help wondering if it was my fault that I seem to attract women who are either convinced there's someone in the shadows or they want to hold my genitals hostage.

She later discovered that I don't have a brother and has threatened to do a lot more with my privates than just grab them next time. What was most surprising about the whole thing is that she's a school teacher...a primary school teacher. They had beards in my day...

At home, and Mitch, Leroy and Marco were standing by the front door chatting. In fact Leroy was seated, balancing on the wall that runs alongside the stairs. A serious and earnest discussion was under way; do they buy cheap beer with their collective savings, or cheap vodka? The decision seems to be between drinking the whole evening or getting some vodka and therefore off their faces a lot quicker. To make his point Leroy, forgetting that he was using his hands to hold on, demonstrated the size of the vodka bottle that they could jointly afford. He fell. The actual fall (about twenty feet) was silent...the landing, unfortunately was not. Leroy's twenty stone frame hit the floor with such a noise that I can only imagine it is what a cow sounds like when it falls over sideways. The lady who lived below came running out with her hands over her mouth screaming 'oh my God!' over and over while we took the slower route than Leroy had opted for and went down the stairs.

He was prostrate on his front with his head in a bush and groans coming from his mouth. Fortunately no broken bones and the bang on the head would probably have done him a favour. He did go back that evening with a bottle of wine for our badly shaken neighbour; apologising (as I'd insisted he should) for landing in her garden without having asked permission. We were sniggering upstairs as we listened.

FRIDAY OCTOBER 1st 2010

I've just a read recent survey, while sitting in a beachfront café, (there's something so 'expat' about listening to the waves, crash, glasses clink and the distant shouts of a bored bingo caller) which informed me that many of the foreigners (especially the Brits) have taken to exercising, specifically walking, since they have made the move to Spain.

Sorry, but no…that is just not happening. You only have to look around the Urb's at this time of year and you'll see expats 'exercising'. Cheeks puffed out and with a sweatband on their wrist they don't often get much further than the first bar they come across and it is there they can 'get out of this heat' and rest up for a while….with a beer. The same happens on the return journey when possibly two more pints are sunk before Daffy waddles back down the hill and looks forward to the cool air-conditioned house that was left on earlier in preparation for his return. And the fridge. For in the fridge lie more beers, and possibly that half a cow that Daffy couldn't quite find space for last night.

It looks good – all these people getting out in the fresh air, leaving their old life back in the UK and thinking, for once about their health….or it could it be that most of them have lost their licence to drink-driving since their arrival…..or am I just being a git…?

But those that have fallen into the common habit of having a few beers and driving home have also felt the full force of the law and a brush with the law in Spain can be a harrowing experience… but as I wrote earlier it can also be a very useful one depending on who you know…i.e. the police chief..?

This time I was stopped by the local Police (the 'Locals') on my motorbike whilst going up a one-way street, the wrong way, and without a helmet. Fortunately for me it was my mate Paco and he just fancied a chat. He didn't even mention my driving.

The Cozzers, Filth, Fuzz, Bill, call them what you like but just don't do it in Spain. Although if you're a friend of the 'Locals' you'll get along fine because your local police officer is the difference between getting a parking ticket (and towed away immediately) or parking where the bloody hell you like. For example, in the small town of Santa Pola near to where I live and the venue, more often than not, of my breakfast each morning, they have built an underground car park. Not just any car park mind you – this one involved tunneling under the town's crown jewel, the castle. Sixteen million Euros and two years of disruption went into creating underground parking spaces for just three hundred cars.

So what do we do in the mornings when we need somewhere handy to park? We park on top of it. Yellow curbs dictate that we will get towed away and fined but that's where Juan (another Local Policeman) comes in. Because he is on the same shift every day – he eats his breakfast at the same place at the same time each day, and therefore so do I. Buy him a coffee, give him a slap on the back and ask nicely if it's ok to leave the car there for a bit and he'll nod and tell you not to worry about it. He even once guided me into a parking space that was only meant for motorbikes but he just moved a few and told me 'no rush' as I ran in the bank.

However the Locals have got a bit of a reputation in Spain for, well, not doing a lot actually. They are the Spanish that you hear about before you come to live in Spain – they are the 'Locals', which means they are the most laid back coppers in the world. Yes they carry a gun, but I've yet to meet one who has actually drawn it in anger and even the chief of police (who happens to be the brother of the Mayor) is of the same breed. A meeting in his office ended in a bar down the road and when I asked him what time he finished his shift - as we supported each other in an effort to navigate the exit – he informed me that it was just about to start. Another tale is of a young man I know who, as is very common, was stopped while he was walking along the street one evening and searched by the Locals. When they discovered some marijuana in his possession they drove him away…to the beach, where they asked him to roll one, which all three in the car shared.

They're never in a hurry and tend to have a habit of getting in the way of the Guardia Civil. No more so than just last week when having had reports called through to me at my news desk of four abandoned boats left on the shore overnight, the Guardia, fearing a town full of illegal immigrants raced to the scene with lights blazing and sirens blaring. The national police were right behind them too, adrenalin pumping, pistols drawn and serious looks on their faces. But, unfortunately for them the Locals had got going first and as these two police forces tried to make haste by belting down the narrow roads towards the location of the immigrants, they were hampered by the local police car in front, with the driver poodling along – one arm out of the window, and whistling… imagine Officer Dibble from Top Cat walking along and twiddling his truncheon while whistling and you get the idea.

THURSDAY OCTOBER 7th 2010

I stayed in on my own last night, on the sofa with some goodies a DVD and a box of tissues (it was a sad film before you go down that train of thought...) but today I'm out and about.

I need a new phone; the trouble is you just can't trust the Spanish to give you honest advice on what's the best buy for you. That is, of course, if anywhere is open as in October half of my town tends to shut until, say, Easter. But the sales staff, if you get lucky, will tell you whatever you want to hear. Or have you already been shopping in Spain? Of course you have...it's best described as 'challenging' at times, I think. No matter if you're buying a screwdriver or a whole new wardrobe (either kind) you will have your patience tested to the limit by an 'assistant' who is an 'expert' not only in producing a face full of zits, but also in whatever their current employer sells. After selling you a new suit (that doesn't fit) be assured that you can return home with your purchase safe in the knowledge that last week that salesman was working elsewhere...asking customers, 'do you want chips with that...?'

Ask them about having something in stock and you may as well have asked if you could bugger their pet Labrador for all the help you'll get. The first thing that they'll do, when the sales assistant has finished talking to her mate and offered you a few moments of her valuable time, is look at the shoe that you'd like to try on (but in a size above pigmy) and walk back to exactly where you have been searching while she's been on the blower and look around for a bit before telling you what you already know. At this point you ask if they may have some in stock. In the back maybe? Again, the Labrador look appears on her face until it dawns on her that there could be a remote chance that they have more than one pair of each shoe, so off she trots.

Now is the time to take a rest or read a good book because she won't be back for what seems like weeks and you know, you just bloody well know that, after waiting so long that several prime ministers have come and gone, you will be disappointed. And in that respect they never let you down. Back she comes, looking slightly older, with a box containing shoes - so far so good - and the right size, things are looking up, until you open it and find a completely different shoe to the one you'd hoped to see.

'But it's the same size Señor…?'

They're not too partial to being discreet either, one time I went into the farmacia to buy some condoms and was a bit concerned that the young girl who worked there might be serving and that it would be a little embarrassing for both of us. I let out a long breath when the male owner of the business came behind the counter, so I moved in and placed my order. Only for him to walk off for his lunch and shout – because quite a few customers were talking – to the young girl and anyone else in earshot that the Englishman wanted some condoms…but only a small pack…

It didn't get any better the next day when I went to the bodega to get some wine because as I pulled out my wallet one of the much announced condoms flew out and across the floor in front of the female owner. Trying to make light of it I laughed, while she gave me a look that said she had a Labrador…and was worried…

I love living here and I love the Spanish people but some things are just very hard to try and get used to…I can't help feeling that us Brits are dreaming the Spanish dream but are better designed to live in Middlesborough…

WEDNESDAY OCTOBER 6th 2010

Bertie and Wooshter are back, Herrs Flick are off elsewhere talking to other goat-fearing people, so our chat had nothing to do with animal abuse this time, No today was all about how the 'virgin' Mary and Joseph arrived at the stable on a donkey and crashed out for the night. My argument that no man in his right mind was going to believe that she was up the duff through Immaculate Conception – and the sperm donor looked like Father Christmas – didn't go down too well. Nor did the one about how ironic it was that Jesus was a carpenter and was put to death on a wooden cross. Or the point I made about Mary Magdalena, allegedly, being a prostitute. I was in one of those sorts of moods. And I think they realised, as they set off…telling me God would save all. Yeah right, except for a Chris Waddle penalty – which he wouldn't need to would he? (Was I in a bad mood or what..?)

As I've said before, nothing should surprise you once you begin living in Spain and last night was no different.

As part of my work for the magazine, I'd thought a while ago that it would be a good idea for my son and I to learn to Scuba Dive. Two reasons really, it'll make an interesting article with some nice photos and secondly, because I just wanted to.

Pete and Louise, my instructors from Birmingham have been together, working and matrimonially, for years and were guiding us along the way with lessons that we managed to fit in around working. Nothing surprising there, I hear you say, but hang on. I'm sitting in a bar last night on the roof terrace, enjoying a quiet pint and my own company, again. This was one of those 'chill-out' style places with just candles for lighting and dark corners to get lost in. As the soft jazz filled the background, I heard a voice from out of the darkness.

'DAVE!' I look up. No one there.

'OI! DAVE!' again nothing.

This was getting weird. I returned to reading my paper thinking that maybe four pints on an empty stomach had fitted me nicely with a pair of beer goggles and voices calling out to me. Time to go maybe. Before I could finish my fifth, the voice came again.

'DAVE! OVER 'ERE.'

Oh, shit. It's the Indian ice cream lady sitting in a dark corner - I really couldn't see her until she moved into the light of a nearby candle. Now what do I do?

'Y'ALL RIGHT DARLIN'?' she said as she approached.

I replied that yeah, everything was good; all the while frantically looking for an escape route, out of the darkness appeared Pete – the diving instructor – looking rather sheepish.

'I FINK YA KNOW PETE DONTCHA' she said, as Pete slowly made his way over.

Apparently they've been at it for a while amongst the flakes and the chopped nuts. Another expat marriage bites the dust but I guess, on the positive side, another new romance begins – even if it is to the tune of Greensleeves and with a sign on the back, which says 'WATCH OUT FOR KIDS!'

Afterwards I'd headed for home; ready for a good book and an even better glass of red – well at least I got the red.

I think I mentioned that Mrs J has a taste for books. My books. Five at the last count – and don't sit there saying; 'well you should have put them out of the way,' I did. Doors, cupboards, pedal bins and toilet seats (no idea…) can't hold her any more so we have to be extra careful. Looking at me with a mixture of amusement and pity, she bites off chunks and chews yet another best seller as I tell her off yet again…where's the respect…?

THURSDAY OCTOBER 7th 2010

In the morning I took the dogs out for a run on the campo but the Spanish SAS were out in force - -or the *budgie-killers* as they have come to be feared…

It's the shooting season in Spain. For what I'm not entirely sure but they are a bit partial to shooting, or killing in one form or another (so long as it's got fur, feathers or fins), and then eating whatever it might be (no matter how small).

I've seen them in the trees near to our house with their laser scopes and night optics. How come they can get them but the British soldiers abroad can't…? Anyway, they will bead their little red dot on some poor unfortunate rabbit's head before blasting it in the foot and having to use up two or three more hollow points to finish the job properly. All the while dressed as if they are on black ops in Columbia.

When I'm out with the dogs, and these guys are creeping silently through the trees in search of their prey, I call Mrs Jones and Meg just as Jose Rambo is putting the red dot on a sparrow from ten yards. Off flies the bird while its frustrated assassin settles in the hope that some poor rabbit will come limping along.

Mitch and I were invited to go along to a clay pigeon shooting range on the outskirts of Alicante. The chance to hold a gun like his rap heroes was reason enough for Mitch - how is it that these rappers who sing about their life of crime and time spent in jail have done all this and become a famous singer by the time they're nineteen..?

We went and were met by the two brothers who owned the place (top players in the shooting world) and after allowing us to have a go, where we managed a measly one or two out of six each time, Fran and Alberto showed us how it was done by getting fives and mostly sixes in their session. A good day out for Mitch and an article ready to be written so we went home satisfied…and deaf.

MONDAY OCTOBER 11th 2010

Into work at the newspaper today. Ken excelled himself and shot to the top of the league – for idiots. His three sons; Nick who owns the newspaper – and who can do no wrong. Another back in the UK who I haven't had the pleasure of meeting but who Ken describes as 'alright.' Then there's Derek who works at the newspaper. Now Derek does as he's told. Put a camera in his hand and tell him he's a photographer, and he'll take pictures all day. So with Pete out of the picture (pardon the pun), having been inconveniently sacked, it was left to Derek to take over the design and layout of the 'paper – so they gave him an Apple Mac computer and told him to 'design'.

I liked Derek, he would just get on with it and we'd have some great chats about…well about football really because that was his life…just football, but he loved it with a passion. Nice bloke. What really grated was when Ken was talking about his sons with pride until he brought up Derek. From then on he went into an anecdote of how the doctors hadn't realised his wife was pregnant with him and at the time thought he was a cyst. Ken thought it was hilarious…everyone else, including Derek who heard it all, didn't.

After work it was back to the Glorieta Square outside of Juande's café. I sat and had a cigarette while I watched, and listened, to the bedlam around me. Kids (all ages, shapes, colours and with differing amounts of snot dripping from their noses) ran around looking for all the world as if they were out of control. Mum and/or dad were probably around somewhere, chatting over a café with other parents of 'missing kids,' while their parents (Nan with legs at 'ten to two' – why do they *all* do that…?) were elsewhere in the square probably sitting on a bench talking to other wrinklies but never, ever, moaning about the youngsters that ran around them; grabbing their clothes and interrupting the conversations.

A football flew past my head and found its way into a crowd of elderly men, some chewing on cigars, who kicked it around their own feet for a bit as a snotty nose looked on - pleading for it back, and dripping…

Elsewhere two small dogs had been sniffing each other's backsides for so long that they must have known each other's DNA by now and decided that it would be best to chase around the crowded square, barking and causing a bit more havoc, before their owners had had their fill and took them home.

Driving home and I saw that there were two Moroccans at the local bins sweating heavily and drinking water. Beside them sat a very old, very battered and extremely overloaded Peugeot 205 with two women and three kids inside. On its roof a three-seater sofa, an armchair and a wardrobe all tied onto the roof (as there was no roof-rack) with plenty of thick rope. This sort of thing they do every day as a way of earning some money, and good luck to them.

If you've lived in Spain I bet you've done it…I know I, and many others have, but nobody wants to admit to it. Sneaking around, hoping none of our friends will see us but really, we can't help it – the reward is often too good to ignore the opportunity. What am I on about? 'Binning' that's what, and if you don't know what 'binning' is well, you're missing out my friend.

'Binning' is the name given to spotting something you like that's been dropped off at the local bins and going and getting it for yourself. If you did this in the UK, I can guarantee you'd be excommunicated out of the WI or blackballed from the golf club committee but here in Spain its ok…so long as no one knows.

You see, the Spanish have this great concept of not destroying everything that they no longer need or want and, if it's in reasonable condition (depends, of course on how you define 'reasonable'), they'll leave it next to the bins (rather than in it) for someone else to make use of. I know numerous expats who go 'binning', one who even watches from her flat with binoculars so she can get there first, but none are prepared to 'come out' about it. I'm the first to admit that I've found some great furniture that someone else has just grown tired of, and some stuff is even displayed quite well when leaving it at the 'bin supermarket'. Two friends who came out a long time ago in the 'binning world' found a complete, and in perfect condition, lounge suite and promptly furnished their apartment – but they won't say a word about it.

The 'moros' have been at it for years, and making a few quid on the side, and now the good ol' expat is catching on to this environmentally friendly, but curiously shady, way of doing things. I've put stuff down there myself – the unused multi-gym with nothing wrong with it went within seconds.

But in a country where new is good and old is for the scrap-heap it's good to see that in some ways our hosts are way ahead of us. Imagine how much less landfill space would be needed if we all adopted the practice of not just dumping old items to be buried or incinerated, but made them available to others with different tastes, budgets, or larger gardens to take it away. We would then be saving the council money with less trucks on the road, less bin men and less bins…meaning that we will all pay less for our rates next year…oh sorry, drifted off into fiction there…

However, half the stuff that gets picked up next to the bins ends up in markets, or more often a '*Rastro*' (a kind of crap car boot sale…selling well, crap). By the way, if you've never been to a market in Spain then go because markets are fascinating, or more accurately the people at the Spanish markets; at the last one I left with a four foot rug, a diving knife and a pair of 'Ray Ban' sunglasses and the whole lot cost me less than ten Euros. And, at a *Rastro* you can buy anything you want – you name it the Africans have salvaged it from your local bin and put it back on sale; from fridge motors to car tyres and old Hoovers to dildos, the world, as Del Boy used to say, is your Lobster.

The trouble with the markets is you will often find that someone has decided to bring their dog. To a market. Why anybody thinks that taking a pet to the market is a good idea is beyond me.

As you fight your way through the group in front that have decided to stop and have a chat in the middle of the row you inevitably come across the beggar. If it's not one of those east European women who happen to have possession of the family baby for the day and is claiming (even though she must, at best, be the baby's grandmother) that she needs some cash to feed it, it'll be someone with some horrific disability or something. I once went to the local market only to round the corner and there in front of me, on the floor, was a man with no arms or legs, just a tin hanging from his neck which had a piece of paper stuck on it that asked for money. Now I could have stuck one hundred Euros in there but then I got to thinking…*he's* not going to be getting it out later is he? Come to that, how did he get there and how is he getting home? I couldn't believe his family just dropped him off in the morning and promised to be back later to pick him up.

Either he had a really, really, good friend who he trusted to look after his cash or someone else did it for him, I decided against a donation and offered him a drink of water instead which he seemed just as pleased to receive.

But if you're not treading on Yorkshire Terriers or dodging quadriplegics you'll no doubt be arguing with the African woman - reminding her that what hair you have got left you don't really feel is necessary to be braided and as you finally get away from her you'll bump into your neighbours who are out on holiday for the week. Now you feel obliged, even though you've seen them every day of the week so far, to make some mundane small talk, in the middle of the row, blocking all the foot traffic.

I bumped into two retired gents who have been together a long time and come from that time when London was run by the Krays and other gangs. For the simple reason that I don't fancy getting my head kicked in we'll call them the two Rons. I hadn't seen them in a while and as we blocked the row, pinning down a couple of Shiatsu's with our feet at the same time, they asked, if in my capacity as editor of a local magazine, why the TV satellite channels have changed and did I realise the porn is now awful? The two Rons (coming from London) weren't the quietest chaps in the world and declared it a 'fuckin' outrage' that all they got to see was some 'bird takin' it up 'er jacksy' or 'a screen full of muff..' before we moved on to discussing the contentious points in Darwin's theory I made my excuses and promised to do what I could about the porn…

Back home and not content with stealing my dinner, which I'd left on the worktop in the kitchen, Mrs bleeding Jones also spat the peas out, and onto the floor. It wouldn't have been so bad if I hadn't waited forty-five minutes for my son to come back in with his mate and then blame him before realising (yes, I am this thick…) that, A) The knife and fork were clean and, B) Four gravy-coloured footprints led back to the sofa…

Mitch had brought some female friends home again this afternoon and I'd been banned from talking to them. Well, not actually banned but Mitch insisted that I didn't do my usual introduction which involves me enquiring if their mums are ok, and/or married. So I left them to it and got on with cleaning the house.

An hour later and covered in sweat and dirt and dust I began on the stairs that lead down to the pit. As I reached the bottom I could hear Mitch groaning. Fearful of what I might find and remembering that he is entitled to his privacy…. I took a peek. He had one girl massaging his head (that lay in her lap) while the other was rubbing his legs.

'Hiya!' I said as I marched in hoping to make them jump. Not a flinch from any of them just a collective 'hi' back. And a very vague introduction from Mitch as he waved his hands in the general direction of the kitchen and said, 'this is Gemma and Skye.' They were all watching a film.

'How are you? I asked, looking at both of them in turn, to which they informed me that they were 'fine fanks.'

'And how are you parents?'

'Well it's just me and me mum cos they just split up' said Gemma 'but she's fine.' I could have sworn Mitch sighed at this point.

'Really? Well she should come out for a drink sometime,' I offered.

As I reached the top step the mop, launched by Mitch, flew past my head. I was only asking…no respect…I hate kids.

13 THE ART OF WAITING…

THURSDAY OCTOBER 14th 2010

It was a gorgeous October evening but there I was, standing on the local beach, dressed in rubber and waiting for another bloke dressed in rubber to join me. Before you start thinking all the rumours are true, my son Mitch was with me, and we were going diving. And anyway, we were a good few hundred yards away from the 'Stop & suck' drive-in palm grove for gays. In reality I don't think we were going to go out of our depth but by the time this story gets back home…I'll have been searching a wreck for sunken treasure while battling Stingrays and Sharks, and other big wet things.

I'd always wanted to dive – ever since I tried it out in the Caribbean a few years ago with a very dodgy guy who just kept smiling and saying 'all good friend' while puffing on a reefer and that was whenever I asked if doing it with no training at all was strictly legal. But I liked what I saw down there and I'd wanted to do it again, and properly…and safely this time.

This was our first dive, and the plan, apparently, was to bring us back in one piece – which was nice, I thought.

We'd been at the dive school, on the new port in Santa Pola, for a couple of days previously with the instructors. It felt a bit like learning to drive again, but obviously you don't need the goggles and flippers…unless my mum is driving.

We survived the diving, and the barking from the former military officer who was our instructor telling us – and getting very irate doing it I might add – that,

'For the thousandth time! They aren't friggin' goggles and flippers…they're masks and fins…!'

Whatever.

Time to get ready…I'd been invited out…by a lovely Spanish woman no less. A phone call from her and ten minutes later I was showered, changed and ready to go (it shouldn't take as long as that…).

Half an hour later we met in town and went for an aperitif in a quiet bar before moving on to the restaurant - I'd booked it earlier, in-between the shower and getting dressed – and it was here that we bumped into a couple of her friends.

Three hours later and with several other friends and various members of her extended family in tow – and a few more bars patronised - we were within spitting distance of the restaurant. The same restaurant where I'd reserved a table in readiness for a cosy meal for two…and we should have been there two hours previously. But, as usual, when I'm out with a beautiful woman (it happens…ok?) I was not using my brain to do the thinking and had left the restaurant number at home, so it was a case of pacifying the owner when we eventually got there.

We got there at just after midnight. All fourteen of us. And, as ever in Spain, the owner didn't bat an eyelid when asked to make room for another dozen people at the cosy corner table…how romantic.

After another two and a half hours of eating and drinking and more eating, only interrupted by the Spanish family members asking (shouting) me questions – all at once, and the end was in sight – the restaurant was shutting. I got out, stuffed with the finest seafood and the cheapest wine, and with a back looking (and feeling) as if it was severely sunburnt after the whole lot of 'em had slapped me as an affectionate way of saying goodbye. I remember the soccer riots of the eighties and I got slapped more gently by gorilla shaped Arsenal fans back then than I did on this night.

But it was the end, and I could go home. Six hours, and after enough food to make Pat Butcher smile and having consumed liquids designed to test the fittest bladder, it was over…and there was me earlier in the evening just hoping for a quick nibble…

As ever our waiter was hopeless and for a nation full of waiters they are not very good at it are they? In fact they're terrible. Whether you're under the golden arches - ordering something that'll mean you need to buy your next shirt in size XXL, or in a 'Chic' restaurant elsewhere, you can't have failed to notice…that they haven't noticed you.

Observation is not a strong point of our Iberian hosts, how Columbus ever found his way home is a mystery still…unless he just went around Ibiza a few times before coming back? And you only have to look at the quality (or lack of…) driving in this country to realise that unless it's stuck on their windscreen – they won't see it. I'm pretty much convinced now that the Spanish, being a nation of doing what they say, have heard the driving instructor tell them to look when they arrive at a junction…but he never said anything about stopping…

Perhaps there is a gene for peripheral vision that they lack - who knows - but the waiters and, it must be said, waitresses of this land seem to be able to focus on one thing only; on the way out from the bar they'll be looking at the table they are about to serve and on the return journey, they focus on the bar. Just try getting the attention of one of them while they make these trips and you may as well ask Stevie Wonder to finish your crossword. You can shout, wave your arms around, try the polite; 'por favor', 'perdonname', 'Señor (ita)', or ultimately 'OYE!' but all to no avail. Twenty minutes of smiling and pointing the odd finger in the air and you'll be up at the bar trying to place your order, but, because they are so busy serving every other table in the place – you'll have to wait.

No, it seems that the waiters of Spain have sussed out the art of waiting…they make us do it for them, and god help you if you walk in to a restaurant when the owner and his family are having a meal because you may as well put on an apron and cook it yourself, it'll be quicker. Perhaps they've got it right and I'm just impatient, but having been in a group of fourteen, in a not very busy restaurant last night, and waited for twenty minutes for one of the *three* waitresses to notice us – I know I'm right. And what's more they don't even say….'do you want fries with that?'…

If we're talking about waiters then one story I must tell you is of when we first arrived in Spain and bought the house in the middle of nowhere (because it was all we could afford). Our nearest bar was also the local post office and was run by two brothers – the Chuckle Brothers. Not really, but they looked like them and were always polite and had their own TV show…ok they didn't but they could have had. One of them, José, was great and always attentive and helpful. The other, Miguel, was not so great, and always pissed. He'd stand at the end of the bar and when José went off to do something, which was often – relatively speaking – Miguel would down a quick shot. This would continue all day, or until Miguel just collapsed in a heap on the floor, where they would leave him. We booked a meal there one Sunday and Miguel had apparently been appointed as our waiter.

He got our order right, and the drinks, except for a glass of milk that Mitch had ordered. That arrived steaming hot and not chilled as he was used to. No problem, I thought, as I explained to Miguel (whose eyes were focused somewhere about 50 yards behind me) in broken Spanish that he wanted cold milk.

'No pash (hic) nada' (no problem) he said and stumbled off to the kitchen.

He came back with a handful of ice and dropped it into Mitch's drink, saying,

'Ok? Ees cold?'

I said that I thought that Mitch might want it a little colder, hoping that he'd take the hint and go and get a cold milk from the fridge, but no.

'Ees no problema' he said as he raised the other hand and dropped the rest of the ice cubes in.

'Now ees cold.' He confirmed…

Still the food was good and the service was interesting…although we were careful not to tread on Miguel as we left.

SATURDAY OCTOBER 16th 2010

Back to normal which means the Glorieta Square. And a curious, very old, and very scruffy man with an old fashioned camera on a sort of trolley system rolled up and began setting up what best can be described as an instant outdoor studio. He had a sheet on which he had painted some scenery…badly. The locals - being Spanish, and therefore extremely inquisitive - started to converge on him and soon enough they were sold on the idea of an 'old time photo' of themselves…until they saw the first one

'But wait!' he shouted as the disappointed locals trudged back to their tables and benches having witnessed his effort. Disgruntled, our man with the Brownie and the bed sheet pulled out of his jacket pocket the biggest reefer and lit up. In the middle of the square, in full view of the world (and a parked police car – although I know cars can't see…) He puffed away until it was all gone. He looked at the butt, threw it in the gutter, packed up his gear and headed home…

But it's a typical Saturday evening and therefore, the Square is full of families. How the Spanish love their kids, but do they really need to keep them in a pushchair until they're fourteen? In Britain it's a bit different because by the time mum and dad have got back from work having synchronized their BlackBerries, 'networked' over a cup of turd-flavoured dish water, or Starbucks as it's now called, and picked the kids up from the child-minders, there is barely enough time to send them a goodnight text before 'I'm a celebrity big brother talent show' starts on TV.

Yes, the Spaniards have a lot more time for their kids but what is alarming is how long they make them stay kids for. Ok, so in Britain we're teaching them the fine art of wielding a knife by the time they're three and we start looking for friends who have a house near to the school we want them to go to (in 10 years' time). But in Spain it's a bit different. Yes there are thugs, yobs and losers (or the French as they're commonly known) but these youngsters fear no-one.

No-one that is apart from their mother, grandmother, aunty…or their older sister. Do something wrong when out of their sight and one of these will soon find out from a neighbour or friend and then there is hell to pay. These formidable women have a tongue so sharp they can cut you down at twenty paces and a pitch of voice that makes a pneumatic road drill sound like a child's music box. Cross them at your peril because if little (or often, not-so-little) Juan has done something wrong, a dressing down in the local plaza in front of his mates and half the town's population is commonplace. And woe betide the one who answers back because a cuff round the ear followed by a march home is the only reward he'll get.

I'm not sure who's got it right really, the Brits with kids trained in advanced communications and the ability to shave with a machete or the Spanish with children who are still happy to eat with their parents, and be pushed around in a pram until they're ready to start work.

One thing for sure, come the next war I'd rather have the British kids defending us than the Spanish ones, who'll be lined up behind the female members of their family…on second thoughts…

SATURDAY OCTOBER 23rd 2010

Juan, one of my son's 'dodgy' friends was at the house today. He's from Columbia and has always been polite and interesting to talk to but with Juan you have to check that you've still got your watch after you've shaken his hand. Juan's main problem was that while everyone liked him, no one trusted him so work was hard to come by. Ever resourceful though he'd decided to become a painter and decorator and using his talent for sales he soon had a good few jobs lined up. The trouble was he'd employ his mates who he'd drop off at an address with a bucket of paint and some brushes and just point at the house be painted. That was fine, he was after all the boss, but when at the end of jobs he didn't pay the lads he found himself with lots of work but no one willing to do it, for free. That was the end of that little scheme. He's had a few others since which seemed to involve him taking a load of money up front and then going away for a bit. Seemed to work for him.

When I'd arrived home I'd done my chores; walking the dogs and washing up but I fancied an evening sipping cold beer on the roof terrace of a local bar so I thought my friends would probably be up for it.

'Are you coming out?' Said the text that I sent to my good mate, Mark.

'Nah, X-Factor tonight mate, maybe tomorrow', came back the reply.

No worries, I thought I'd try Baz but he replied that it was '*Strictly*' night so no chance. After a few others had blown me out (that means they turned me down in case anyone is thinking I got lucky…) I grabbed a newspaper from the local shop and headed for a roof terrace bar nearby.

I'd not been sitting there five minutes when someone I knew came up to me and asked what I was doing out on a Saturday.

'Don't you watch 'Strictly,"? She asked, as if I was some sort of weirdo…

'No', I responded, 'I've got a life and I can go out whenever I want and do what I want without having a TV schedule dictate my diary', sometimes you have to educate people…

'So have we – we've SkyPlus'd it'. She said.

SUNDAY OCTOBER 24th 2010

I had a bit of a chat with my mate Paco about names – he couldn't understand why many of us Brits have a middle name. The trouble is neither can I, unless it's for parents to pay homage to relatives? Which would explain why some poor little sods are saddled with a middle name like Ethelred or something? However, trying to work out why the Spanish have about fifteen surnames was a little trickier.

Traditionally, in our culture, if Jimmy Brown and Mary Smith, who live in a British culture, decide that it's time to stop their little b*****ds actually being little b*****ds and get hitched, their child/children would adopt the husbands surname and become say, John Brown etc. Exciting isn't it? But bear with me (not literally obviously – they're all hibernating) and we'll get somewhere with this.

The Spanish, on the other hand, being lovers of the written word (why use five words when twenty will fit?), tend to have more than the one surname and at times quite a few. It's not unusual for some to have three or four, in fact a friend of mine is called, Maria Carmen Mendoza Lopez Garcia Ramirez de Garcia. Not so much double-barrel as a Gatling gun of a name – which, come to think of it, it actually sounds like when she says it.

How do they get their names? And in what order is it supposed to go? And, while we're at it, why don't expats out here have surnames? I'll come to that one in a bit but first the Spanish surnames.

The basic rule of Spanish names is fairly simple, when you are born you receive the father's surname (the one from his father) first and the mother's surname – from her father.

For those, like me, that need it hammering home (there's a gag there too…) an example would be, say we have a certain Teresa García Ramirez. Teresa is the name given at birth, García is the family name from her father, and Ramirez is the family name from her mother.

If Teresa García Ramirez then goes and gets up the spout and needs to marry her beau - Elí Arroyo López, she doesn't change her name. But what she would do would be to add "de Arroyo" - making her name Teresa García Ramírez de Arroyo.

Sometimes, the two surnames can be separated by 'y' (meaning "and"), although this is less common than it used to be: Elí Arroyo y López and now and again the grandparents names are thrown into the mix too making really long monikers such as Maria's. It all began because of Arabic influence during the years of the conquest and has stayed as a tradition ever since.

Now to the expats and the vast amount of us who don't seem to have a surname in Spain. I'm talking mainly about Brits but there are a few Spanish too. I myself have been known as 'Jungle Drums Dave' because of the name of my magazine for the last five years and before that as 'car hire Dave.' It seems we're either categorised by our job, or, if not, by our accent. 'Geordie Bob' and 'Essex Steve' are common examples of this trait and it's got to be the way forward hasn't it? That's where we originally got our surnames, but the new versions are much better. Take someone called Cooper for example. With all due respect to all the Coopers out there, it's not very exciting is it? – being named after a barrel. But then take an expat who runs a bar called 'Sunset' and you get 'Tracey Sunset,' what a name eh? Or how about becoming Frankie Carabassi or even 'Quicksave Claire' has a certain ring to it.

The argument falls down a little when you remember that not all possibilities should be explored. i.e. 'Barry Poxy Bar on the Corner' doesn't quite work and there's always people who seem to wear fifteen different hats, the ones whose advert says, 'Local Specialists in Yoga and Spiritual Teachers with over twenty years' experience (also key-holding, dog walking and taxi runs).' We all know at least one, how about 'Del' the Toilet Cleaning Sparky Plumber de la Taxi? We could fit right in to the Spanish culture with names as long as that; in fact they'd probably look at us with a wry respect if we did so.

I saw a couple of belters the other day (insert innuendo here please...), one was a Spanish man who runs a scrap yard and is known, and it'll be either a very good reason, or a very bad one, as 'Chorizo Juan' or sausage John in our lingo which seems to take it in a different direction altogether. But the best, the very best I've heard recently was for a middle-aged Brit who made a Sharpei dog look like it had just been ironed. His name? 'Dennis...whose skin don't fit...'

I left Paco and headed home to find a present from Mrs J who, as you know, has been in our lives for a while now. And with the current state of the planet, I think I, for one, can sleep at night knowing that I am doing my bit to help the environment. You see Mrs J is a green dog – not in colour of course – but in the way she runs my, I mean her life.

She eats everything. I mean everything - from litter in the street to something she ate yesterday, regurgitated back up onto the floor (in front of everyone so we can all see it clearly) and then she will eat it again! Clever eh? And if she doesn't eat it the other one will...they do not waste anything in the animal world. She struggles with plastic bags and shoelaces though – these seem to be returned to the floor, using the aforementioned process, in the same condition as they went in...

Yes, I know that most of what she consumes will generally exit the tradesman's entrance when she's on the campo having a walk but even that is bio-degradable - if it can exist long enough before my other pooch rolls in it. So there you have it get a dog....although I can't vouch for her carbon emissions...perhaps I could get her hooked up to that machine they use to test cars.

THURSDAY OCTOBER 28th 2010

A cold and wet Thursday morning….well for me it was.

'You want me to what!?' I thought it because I couldn't shout it. The reason I couldn't shout it was due to the fact that I was sitting on the sea bed with my air supply firmly wedged in my mouth and several thousand gallons of water between me and Ness, my scuba diving instructor. She wanted me to fill my goggles, sorry mask, half full of water and then breathe out through my nose and the water would magically disappear as it had when she'd demonstrated the skill minutes before. My son, being a clever-arse had already completed the task successfully and now it was me. My turn, and trust me it's certainly a weird sensation letting the water in until it's just below your eyes, but following Ness's instructions I did as requested and, hey presto, a clear mask. I guess that doing this with a heavy cold may hinder the vision somewhat though.

With my mask now thankfully water (and snot) free we took a look around our underwater world and even though we were probably less than fifty feet from the shore, the abundance of marine life going about its business around us was amazing. I'd always considered scuba diving to be something you needed to spend a fair amount of time on a boat for and that is not a good idea in my case – unless you like hearing the name 'Hughie' shouted over and over…

Dried and rested, I was going out for a meal and this time I'd met someone who didn't look like a relative or have a penchant for boiling small mammals. That's wife material in my book. As a bonus Tamsin was gorgeous, talented and desperate (joke)…my kinda woman. The trouble was, so far, I'd managed to put my foot in it several times when it came to small talk including, somehow implying that I wanted to sleep with her mother, insinuating she was a slapper and telling her that I wished I'd slept with more women – yeah, I know. Anyway despite all that we've got along famously so far, although I've yet to be introduced to her mum for some reason, we'll see what the future holds. Rest assured, Fluffy the rabbit is a little more relaxed.

14 WHEN THINGS GO WRONG...

SATURDAY OCTOBER 30th 2010

Whistling my way around the house while I cleared up Mitch's clothes, there was a rap at the door (don't you hate it when black guys are at the door singing...?). sorry... It was my two sandal-wearing worshippers from Holland, Bertie and Wooshter, and I thought I'd better behave a bit better after their last visit so 'hellos' and 'how are you's' out of the way I listened earnestly...while they read from the Watchtower.

The union of marriage was today's theme (oh dear...) and why, when we swear under oath and in front of God, we should honour those vows. I was, at that point in time, twice divorced and looking for a third – so possibly not the best example of what they were talking about. My uncle Melvin's comment at my last wedding didn't go down too well with the in-laws when he stood up at the reception and proclaimed a 'toast to Dave...'cos his weddings are always good...'. Still B and W seemed understanding enough, and, it appears, that the best thing I could do was meet a lady from their church who had lost her husband in a farming accident. No goats involved, (apparently).

I'm not trying to tempt fate for me and Tamsin but I don't know what it is about Spain and relationships but they seem to fail a lot – and not only mine I might add. Is it the beer? The relaxed way of life? Or just something in the water? Whatever it is there is a disproportionate number of people separating, splitting up amongst the expat community. I had one mate who found out his wife was having an affair when he saw her white stilettos sticking out of the back window of his Ford Fiesta (a Ford Fiesta for Chrissake!) but there you go - It always had been a popular old banger...

But, there are so many couples that come over to the Costa and then a little while later – that's it. All over. After sometimes years of marriage (or just being together) the Expat Bug bites one or the other's genitals and off they wander with the woman from the chippy. In addition, there is never a shortage of receptive 'new' partners because this cycle goes on and on all over the Urb's. Marriages have crumbled and handbags have been thrown and all of a sudden, another bar is on the market as one of the couple withdraws their labour along with their love.

Did we all come here with problems already in our relationships or is it really something in the water? Are there really that many couples running away from something (apart from the Inland Revenue, Visa, insert appropriate) that believe that everything will be ok with a 'fresh start'? Yes! If you have not done it yet and your relationship is struggling in the gloomy weather of the UK – what better way to make things perfect again than by changing the one thing that is bound to restore said relationship to your previous wedded bliss – the weather! Thousands come out to the Costas secure in the belief that if they can just move to another country all will be well in the matrimonial department. The fact that the sun is shining and therefore the beaches, streets, restaurants etc. are filled with fit (not always the case...) and tanned men and women - who will fill the bars come the evening – seems not to be a consideration for those who have had problems with a wandering partner before.

People revert to type, I don't care what anyone says, and before too long the old rumour mill grinds away and Mick and Mary are the subject of speculation and gossip.

There are some things you can do on an Urb as a single person and some that you cannot. For example having a coffee with a person of the opposite sex means that you are definitely shagging her. Give her a lift and you will be engaged and a meal out is considered the same as taking your wedding vows. If you really want people to get their sunburnt tongues wagging – take someone shopping. I did it once and never again. The poor woman, and her husband, were not too pleased by the time it reached them that she and I had moved in together. Luckily, hubby knew me better than that –he still lived with her – and a fat lip was avoided.

If your relationship is dodgy – if you have to keep an eye on him or her – do not come to the Costas (or any other foreign clime for that matter). The weather will not make it better or make him or her behave, in fact, it will do the opposite and within a few months, you will be on your own. Or maybe that's what you want? In that case, don't let the other half see this page and tell 'em of the new freedom you can both experience.

As they say, every cloud has a silver wotsit and I suppose even this emotive subject has one too? You see, with all these people separating (whether they wanted it or not) and hooking up with new partners – people are getting a new life in a new place, and the weather's not bad…and of course your new partner wouldn't dream of doing that to you…

But if it all goes tits-up (literally sometimes…) you'll need a lawyer – probably you'll end up with a Spanish one and here I offer a tad of advice because they are generally and to put it bluntly, shit. Now don't get me wrong and before I get writs from the Spanish lawyers association I'm not saying they are all rubbish, just most of them. I'll give you an example of an experience I had with a lawyer in Spain when I was going through my divorce.

With money being tight and my son living with me I had to make sure we had enough money at a time when everything was going up in the land of the cheap and a son that had three hobbies, eating, sleeping and eating some more. So, trying to plan ahead and make sure that I could actually afford said lawyer I asked him to tell me exactly what it would all cost to make sure I put the money aside.

MONDAY NOVEMBER 1st 2010

'Juan I don't want it,' I said as I stared at the fifteen foot wide umbrella and the table and chairs laid out underneath it which he had set up (at some point before I woke up) on my patio and what he was now relaxing in.

'Oh come on Señor Dave – it is very cheap, special price just for you.'

'It was very kind of you to think of me Juan, but for one thing it takes up the whole terrace and really it should go back to where you got it from.'

'No, ees mine!' he insisted as I turned over a chair to reveal the crest of our local town hall underneath.

He went, insisting that he would return them (under the cover of darkness) that very evening, unless he found someone to sell them to first, I'm sure someone, somewhere was having to stand up at whatever function these had been intended for.

I headed off to Torrevieja and work and ended up stuck in the newspaper office all morning, but I fancied an early day. Luckily, for me at least, the opportunity presented itself when one of the two British expats on the local council died suddenly; he'd only been in office a few months. Lenny Marks had been elected in May but had suffered some controversy recently and to hear of him passing was a bit of a shock. taking advantage of the situation I tried to get away (and on the beach) early and told Ken and Nick that I'd set up a meeting with the other expat on the council, Bill

Meeching, for an exclusive interview and as planned, I left a good two hours before everyone else and within twenty minutes of getting home, I had hit the beach and was chilling out on the sand.

A few missed calls from the office was usual but when I did eventually look at the phone and saw that Ken had called over fifteen times I knew something was up. I racked my brain but couldn't think of anything important I'd forgotten, so I rang him. He answered on the first ring and went into a diatribe about honesty and professional ethics before getting to the point. It turned out that we'd got some duff information in the morning and we'd got the name wrong – it was the other councilor who had died. The one I'd, supposedly, made an appointment with. I think Ken's query was; 'how the fuck did you make an appointment with a dead bloke?!'

I carried on working there another year after that…good staff are so hard to come by…

THURSDAY NOVEMBER 4th 2010

A fresh November morning, unusual for Spain, but some things are quite common all year round like when I come out of the house and open the gate to find one stray dog on top of another with its tongue hanging out of the side of its mouth and sweat pouring from its forehead. The one below (presumably female) has a look of resigned indifference on her face and is checking her nails while Rex gives it all he's got. There's got to be a better place for romance but apparently my gate has something going for it.

Bertie and Wooshter were there and trying to 'calm them down' by nudging the top one with their feet but that was a bit like poking a tiger with a broom handle as 'Rex' kept snapping at their sandals.

But this, I've found over the years, is just another day in Spain because if you look around you it's going on everywhere. I don't mean 'Rex' is trying to have his way with everything from a Pekinese to a Brazilian, I mean that everywhere you look there is something 'different' going on. Although sticking with the canine world a Yorkshire terrier moonwalking along the pavement was impressive until I realised it was trying to 'cover' its number 2's, which were about fifteen feet away by now.

I headed for Santa Pola in the car and got stuck behind a guy pushing a shopping trolley up a hill…with two dogs in it (not Rex, or his partner) and at the top a prostitute sat in her beach chair wearing a skirt apparently made from one single piece of duct tape and proved the theory that women are more dexterous than us blokes by impressively eating 'Pippas' (sunflower seeds), chewing gum and smoking all at the same time.

In Santa Pola itself I followed a van that insisted on having right of way over something coming the wrong way up the one way street towards him. He eventually forced them into a space between two parked cars by continually edging closer and closer. The fact that the other 'vehicle' was an elderly guy being pushed in a wheelchair by his equally elderly wife - because Spain's pavements are so narrow they must have been built for unicycles – seemed lost on the van driver who roared past…

Choosing a parking space is always a little tricky though…if I park in one of the diagonals alongside the road, there's a (very) good chance I'll come back to find the colour, and imprint, of someone else's door on my car. Whereas if I go for the street 'parallel parking' option I could find both my bumpers on the floor when I return. I once came back to a couple changing their baby's nappy on the bonnet of my car; theirs was parked next to it…

Anyway, I parked in town and left the guy in front enough room to swing an oil tanker without using my car to bounce off, hopefully, and headed up the road.

'¿Tienes tobaco por favor?'

A man appeared next to me, Spanish and reasonably dressed, and smiling politely. That's another thing to get used to (The Spanish see nothing wrong in scrounging a fag from a stranger). I smiled back and said that I was sorry but I had run out and was on my way to get some - to which he kindly offered to accompany me. He did, and waited outside until I came out and gave him not one, but two (he did ask nicely) cigarettes before he disappeared.

The next thing to happen was I dropped my car keys – no there wasn't a drain – this was a little more awkward than that because firstly they got stuck on the bottom of a blind man's walking stick. I think he may have been a little hard of hearing too as he wouldn't stop when I asked or even acknowledge I was there. A little thought was needed. I got in front of him on my knees and with locals looking on in horror I tried to grab them quickly form the stick as he banged it along the road. That was when they fell...and went between his shuffling feet. Now they bounced from foot to foot as he made his way up the street and unless I was going to take him out like a prop forward- I wasn't going to get my keys. Luck, for once, was on my side, however, as he went into a café and sat down. Although bending down between his legs drew some serious looks...

A quiet evening out shouldn't throw up too much excitement as I was off for dinner in the campo with some friends. The only person going that I didn't know was the German man who was giving me a lift, he was called Fred.

Fred duly arrived, bang on time as you would expect, in a Suzuki car that had possibly been previously owned by Coco the Clown. The passenger door swung open on left-handed bends, meaning I had to grab hold of a laughing Fred (who hadn't warned me) to stop myself ending up with a face full of gravel. And at a junction we had to stop and wait while Fred untangled the make-shift radio aerial - a piece of wire laying across the top of the dashboard - from the steering wheel, which was also, apparently, hilarious.

Still, we got there in one piece (can't say that for the car) and were met by our host. A host, it turned out, who couldn't stop herself from laughing all the time or from dancing to every new song that came on the stereo. Add to the mix the fact that she had a sausage dog called Lancelot (who was addicted to lemons) and a Parrot that said 'Puta!' (whore) every time you walked past it and you have, pretty much, an average night (and day) out in Spain…

The next morning was spent (that should be wasted) in my local bank - where charm is a foreign currency…

FRIDAY NOVEMBER 5th 2010

You know banks. Important places that do important stuff and with staff who have to handle thousands of Euros per day without actually robbing any (mostly). The banks are one of the oldest institutions in the world and the people entrusted to work there are highly respected…except in Spain. And is it any wonder when they treat you like something they've just trod in?

Now, before you think that this is a rant because I've been turned down for a loan or overcharged, or something. Forget it. I've got no particular gripe with the banks, all I have is my experience in dealing with them for the last ten years and I'm not having a go at all the banks either – just mine. To be more specific, my local branches of this particular savings bank which have obviously been using the 'Last Chance' recruitment company to employ their staff.

Firstly, and I know people will be able to associate with this, why is it that on a Monday morning when customers want to access their accounts to pay bills, check balances or resolve problems, they have one person attending the customers? I went in the other day to be greeted by a line of people so miserable from waiting that they would have looked more at home in the eighties election posters for the Tories that proclaimed 'Labour isn't working'. One girl was serving, the other putting up posters… but, I needed to pay a bill so waiting was the only option. I waited, and waited. Finally having celebrated a birthday and an anniversary I was offered a seat at the counter. Fantastic, after all this time I was finally going to get a few things sorted out and still have time to enjoy what was left of my retirement. But then the usual happened. If you've been to my particular bank you'll know exactly what happened next because it always does…yup, the phone rang. Rather than upset the client on the phone who had waited all of a nanosecond for his call to be attended, the cashier answered. So here I am waiting once again as Mr. 'Important' on the phone gets to sort his problems out without the inconvenience of 1. Getting off his arse, and 2. Queuing. All the while I can see his account details, which the cashier has conveniently brought up on the screen for all to consider.

After a while the phone is hung up and another customer is satisfied…but not this one. I needed to pay my phone bill, amongst other things, but as I've missed the 'window of opportunity' I couldn't pay it there and then and would have to wait until tomorrow. I've tried telling Telefonica (who own my line) that too but they just laughed, and cut me off. While I considered what to do next she answered the phone again.

I asked the manageress once I had finished with the cashier if there was any way she could allow me to pay the bill 'out of hours' to save me the inconvenience and cost of getting disconnected. She just carried on chewing her gum while looking at me as if I was the love child of Jordan and Gary Glitter.

I could go to another branch you say? But have you been there? The other branch of this bank is where Mr Charisma-bypass works. I don't know his name but it must involve 'grim' somewhere along the line. He is the most miserable, unhelpful, ignorant person I think I've ever met – and I'm being kind there. The other day I went in (it was empty of clients) and asked if he could tell me my balance.

'You can do that in the machine', he said, while cleverly saving energy by not raising his eyes to look at me.

So off I trotted like a good little boy and got the balance from the machine. I now needed to pay some money in so back I went to Mr. C to do just that. The trouble was I'd left my card in the ATM. When I told him this he (and he really did) sighed loudly, looked at his colleague, rolled his eyes and without a word to me walked off to retrieve it. The rest of the transaction continued without further complications, in fact without another word too because bypass-boy had obviously trodden on his toy trumpet or something that morning. I would have respected him more if he'd said about the card, 'you've done what you moron!?'

Try it out, pop into my local branch and you'll be treated like royalty….Tsar Nicolas the third springs to mind…

THURSDAY NOVEMBER 11th 2010

A life spent hopping from café to café is interesting - trust me; how about the young couple sitting opposite me – all loved up and staring deep into each other's eyes?

As I write they're holding hands and sneaking the odd kiss. One of them is running a hand along the others thigh while they brush hair out of each other's faces, and they say romance is dead. Not according to these two who have just begun a serious game of tonsil tennis in front of the whole place. Romantic? Not for me…but then again they are both fellas…

However, talking of romance, I did have a nanosecond of optimism a bit later when I had an encounter with some ladies, who were visiting the area on holiday. As I was quietly supping my beer on the rooftop bar they walked past where I was seated. All of a sudden whispers started and I overheard 'it's him'. Feeling smug for a humble magazine editor I sat in quiet satisfaction and finished my drink as more guests arrived at their table and began taking furtive looks in my direction. I couldn't help feeling rather chuffed that someone had recognized me…until one of them came over and asked for my autograph, which I duly signed. To say the lady was gutted would be an understatement but then again her repost left me feeling like I'd been kicked in the privates too… 'So you're not Phil Tufnell then…?'

MONDAY NOVEMBER 15th 2010

'He's on the phone again…!' shouted Donna from the other office.

Everyone who has lived in Spain knows the odd 'dodgy' person live here. Keeping their head down and living under a different name, and many more having served their time back home, or 'got away with it' and living in peace out here. Most of these people, despite their history, are reasonably intelligent, I know because I met a lot of them in my role as a newspaper editor on the coast. I also met some, shall we say, not so smart ones too. Top of the pile comes the clairvoyant Simon.

Now Simon had been to our newspaper offices and my colleague had written a profile on him as, being new to Spain, he was trying to attract customers. He'd also discussed with her the possibility of writing an article and answering readers' questions concerning loved ones that had snuffed it – he didn't put it like that, but I did.

Simon was desperate for as much publicity as he could get to get his 'business' going and asked about a late night slot on the radio station that was connected to the newspaper, discussions began. Every day for the next two weeks he called the office to see what was happening, even when we told him we'd need a couple of weeks to get things organized he would call the next day, and the next.

Finally one of the girls in the office who had been dealing with him snapped and refused to talk to him anymore because he was so 'pushy' so the task of dealing with the medium, or at other times his PA, John, fell in my lap. I decided to slow things down a little and asked him to send me his credentials and any testimonials that he may have had from previous clients. He went on to tell me that he was to appear on local TV (I'd spoken to them and they had agreed to interview him) and that any info' that I needed could be found on his website – 'just Google my name'. So I did.

Top of the Google list amongst a load more articles about Princess Di was a piece from the Daily Mail about him. I clicked on it expecting to see something turgid about this amazing medium. It wasn't. It was a report about Simon, with a picture, informing the world that this guy and his accomplice had skipped the country after being found guilty of defrauding a guy for twelve thousand quid. He hadn't even changed his name or his shirt judging by the photo of him in the Daily Mail.

As I say, he hadn't even bothered (or didn't have the intelligence) to change his name. His colleague, at least, had tried although an unimaginative 'John' had replaced Tom and it wasn't long before we heard that he'd been shipped back to enjoy the next three years at the pleasure of Her Maj', bless her.

The good news (for most of us) is that Pete's back. Nick lost the case and has been forced to re-employ him. He is not a happy bunny and won't even talk to Pete; preferring to send messages via staff rather than go to the effort of growing a backbone and doing it himself. So now we've got Donna sticking pins in a Humpty Dumpty doll (pretending its Nick) and Pete quite smugly (and rightly) sitting behind his desk – back at his old job.

What a great job I've got - getting to watch this lot pan out. On top of that we've got Nick's German wife marching around the office demanding that advertisers pay on time.

She asked Pete, who sits next to the printer, to pass her an invoice that she'd printed off.

'Can't', said Pete.

'Vat do you mean "can't" – it is right next to you?'

Pete pulled out his contract and pointed to the relevant paragraph and with a smirk replied, 'says here I'm a designer, so that's all I can do- design, sorry.'

She fumed muttering (I may have heard 'goat' mentioned)…and got it herself. The rest of us just smiled. I'd always hoped it'd be interesting working on a newspaper.

15 MRS JONES MEETS THE GUARDIA...

MONDAY NOVEMBER 22nd 2010

My latest relationship has failed – When Tamsin's daughter started calling me 'Dad' the first time we met it was worrying, but when she introduced me to her new mates as her new dad I knew the mum had been making some serious plans for the future. It was time to close that chapter. (Did I really just write that?).

But the good news is I've met a new girlfriend, the rose-tinted specs are on (again) and the mind has forgotten that one all-important rule; women are very different to us men. Setting aside the obvious physical ones that is – they basically come from another planet don't they? I'm not having a go ladies, as quite clearly, we are different. For example you look at a pile of washing and think 'oh, my god'. We men look at it...and ...well we don't do any more than that. But we differ so much, for example she will say, 'does my bum look big in this' – which it maybe does, and a question to which there is no correct answer. She will then (casually) inform you that, 'yes I have thrown out that tatty old shirt', your favourite.

The trouble with women is that they know when to say the right thing. If things were turned around and we asked them about our bum size the ladies (being smarter than us) would reply with something like, 'it doesn't matter if it does darling, it looks lovely to me,' and we'd go 'oh, thanks'.

Now fellas just try that one out and see if they respond with a loving hug and a 'you say the right things darling.' They won't…what they will do is call you a patronizing son of unmarried parents. Trust me; the females of the world were put on this planet to keep the male population on its toes…and what a fine job they do.

Having said all that, where would we be without them? Forget the obvious and look beyond that - for without them we wouldn't have discovered radiotherapy, the civil rights movement in the US would not have moved on if Rosa Parks had moved to the back of *that* bus, and you wouldn't be getting those lovely Yorkshire Puds from Aunt Bessie…

But I reckon I must be cursed by females (or just really bad at interacting with them). Whether human, animal or vegetable.

Why does she have to do it? And always in front of guests…it drives me mad but come what may, no matter what time of day or night, never mind that she's just been for a long walk to do all the necessaries and smell as many turds as is possible in thirty minutes (there's probably a website dedicated to it somewhere…) she has to do it in front of guests.

Many a time I've had 'company' like last night (well, a few times) and just as the DVD is getting going and the wine is warming the bodies and loosening the tongues. Just as the candles are burning down and you've made *that* move and snuggled up a tad closer….along comes Mrs Jones, across the front of the TV, dragging her backside along the rug, with the most satisfied of grins on her face. Having not murdered the moment enough at this point she will then turn around and sniff along her recent route whilst enthusiastically wagging her tail. Man's best friend….My arse…well, hers really.

THURSDAY NOVEMBER 25th 2010

I got a mild revenge when I got Mrs Jones inoculated for Rabies this morning, Rabies? Mrs Jones? What a waste of money that was – she's always running around the house with wild staring eyes and foaming at the mouth, a little dose of Rabies would probably go unnoticed and I seriously challenge the idea of Rabies taking hold in a country like Spain anyway. I mean, can you imagine? The disease reaches the Spanish border with packs of wild dogs roaming and fighting and chasing everything that crosses their path. They then reach the 'checkpoint' and pass on the disease to the resident Spanish strays who have just had an afternoon's siesta and are preparing to wind down for the evening with a late meal in the usual alleyway followed by a good night's rest curled up with friends. Now I could be wrong about this but I can see the Spanish mutts opening one eye, to witness their French cousins snarling and frothing, as they themselves lay basking in the sun and rejecting the rabies route as far too energetic. Have you seen any rabid dogs around here lately? I didn't think so…you see the theory holds up and goes one step further, you see, give it a few years and 'Yuppie Flu' may well make it to the Iberian peninsula and I can see it now, a pack of Spanish dogs cocking their heads to one side as news of the lethargic disease reaches them and their thoughts turning to: 'now *that's* a disease…'

FRIDAY NOVEMBER 26th 2010

An afternoon at the Newspaper, with Ken having all the festive spirit of Scrooge and refusing to put the aircon on even though everyone, including him, is sweating. In fact he's probably contributing more to the growing floor puddles than the rest of us. Anyway, a bit of research (on the computer, and not on a bar stool unfortunately) looking up booze for next week's feature   kicks out some interesting facts.

According to another survey in one of the 'papers, the more successful you are - the more likely you are to turn to drink. If this is true, and I have no reason to doubt it, then I have the privilege of living amongst some of the most successful people in the world. Another survey (this is obviously the business to be in) declared that the average adult is drinking over his/her weekly allowance and will be liable to suffer the consequences in the form of ill health in the future. Yet another stated that we all eat too much red meat and will lead us to an early coronary (although what James Bond has got to do with it I don't know). It seems we need to watch what we eat and drink but as one of my neighbours says, 'I don't drink more than my daily allowance – I'm just a few years ahead…'

I'm out with Nicole for an early Christmas meal, and she's in a bad mood… Bloody PMT! As you can probably gather, I've just been suffering from a bout of it, by proxy (thanks to Nicole – and we're only friends), and it just stuns me that she can turn from Julie Andrews into Rose West, and back again, in the space of a week. One minute we're holding hands, eating sandwiches on the beach and saying smoochy things in each other's ears and the next I'm locked in a Mini with a Tasmanian devil, that's pissed off. All rhyme or reason disappears at this time of the month – I may as well try discussing child birth with the kettle. A typical situation might go something like, she says,

'Where's the milk?'

I reply, 'In the fridge darling',

She will the respond with 'Agh! Don't worry I'll get it!'

I have no chance, of either understanding or getting it right, or even saying the right thing because as far as I can tell for one week each month – she wants to kill me, slowly. For that seven days or so she holds me responsible for all that is wrong in the world, (which I'm informed is correct)

and her life and for pretty much anything she cares to choose because PMT gives her every damn right to, apparently.

It wouldn't be so bad if it was just 'Tosser!' now and again, I'm used to that, but somehow, and I don't know how, she manages to then persuade me (having chewed my nuts off earlier) that it was in fact my fault that she needed to shout at me earlier and that some way of 'making it up' would be appreciated. Like taking her for an expensive meal or putting that shelf up because it will somehow, 'make everyone's lives easier'.

Easier? For one week a month I'm the equivalent of Charles Hawtry up against Mike Tyson.

Somebody needs to stand up to her and tell her that she can't treat me like it anymore. It's just not gonna be me.

My neighbour Reg popped round this morning to get me to call Telefonica for him as he can't speak Spanish and Telefonica…well…they're just crap to deal with really, especially if you try and speak English to them.

Reg is what I call a survivor in Spain and I couldn't think of a better name for these type of people because survive is exactly what they do. They're Brits – expats who have lived in Spain for a fair amount of time but differ from those that have integrated in (any way) in one way in particular – they just don't fit in. That might seem a strange thing to say but, quite honestly, they don't. They shouldn't be living here, or anywhere else outside of the UK because that is where they truly belong. They also don't seem to be able to grasp the concept that this is a different country, and not theirs.

These are the people that have never mastered the language (neither English nor Spanish sometimes…) and never will, either through lack of ability or they just can't be bothered but somehow, they get by. Usually that's by relying on a friendly Spanish neighbour who can speak another language – even though he doesn't live in a foreign country -

or by visiting various local shops and businesses until someone will help and read the phone bill for them.

The fact that Spain speaks another language doesn't seem to have been considered by the survivor before they emigrated here and the standard survivor statement of *'and they didn't even speak English…'* after they've been fined for a motoring offence seems to imply that the Spanish police force are actually the ones who are a bit slack with their linguistic skills.

They'll normally work in a mate's bar or run a business using their British car, for a while anyway, until one or the other goes bust and they move on. They move on to another mate, or set up another business. I say 'set up' but these people are never going to register at Companies House. Their idea of setting up a business is getting the kids to design some business cards for the latest venture and posting some badly spelt flyers around the locality that some poor unsuspecting mug will respond to. The flyers can be pretty interesting on their own; one of my favourites was for a financial management 'company'. It read, *'Trust us with your savings'*…call Trish or Pete…' it only carried a mobile number and was sellotaped to the wall in a café on photocopy paper, and was (badly) handwritten. Still I'm sure they'll bring my money back soon…

Spain to them is, and always will be, a foreign country not a home. The Spanish, to them, are lazy, ignorant, rude and downright unreliable – except of course their friendly neighbour who, being the exception to the rule is 'not like the Spanish'. Pretty much everything the Spanish do is wrong and backward and they could do with learning a thing a two from the British way of doing things – which is of course the proper way.

And at the end of the day, when it all goes belly up and they can't find a job, or the police have impounded the 'company' car, they head home (UK, of course) because Spain has 'nothing to offer' them. Whereas the going 'home' to the UK has benefits, literally, and most importantly

English speaking people (although too many of them are 'foreign').

They've taken what they could from Spain without giving anything back and the words 'tax' and 'legal' might as well be Spanish too for all the notice they're given, but to the 'survivors', they feel they have been let down and must return. They come and they go, but there are always some of the survivors around, and they are all so similar it's scary. Beware of the survivor when you visit these shores and if you're wondering how to spot them, it's not too difficult - they'll be the ones saying how 'unfair' it was… That's got something else off my chest.

Having said all that, and I can't speak for all nationalities, although I'm sure it's true of them too, but us Brits are a resourceful lot aren't we? Come the day when Obama La Bamba confuses the 'auto-flush' with the 'Nuke-'em' and it all kicks off – I want to be surrounded by my fellow countrymen and preferably in a foreign country.

The Brits (especially the Scottish for some reason) have long been known as a nation of eccentrics who are often found to be keeping late hours in the shed knocking something out. Steady, what I mean is that for centuries Britain led the world in ideas and inventions. Take those same people out of the country and put them in a nice place like Spain - where imagination and inventiveness is often a necessity. And once again, we're in a class of our own. Have a look around and although you won't see the new 'Dyson' or a new type of Hovercraft being tugged out of the garage, what you will see is people who have re-invented themselves and adapted to their new surroundings.

Many of us still need to work out here and have come up with a supply where there is a demand. Everybody knows someone who has come out to Spain and, within a short space of time, set up a property management business or as a builder, mechanic, or even opened a bar or shop. Most of the time these people had no idea, or plan, to end up doing what they are doing. But hats off to us I say – for giving it a go – and getting out there and getting busy. As I say I can't speak for all nations but I wouldn't mind betting the Italians wouldn't fancy it and the French? Well they'd be too busy trying to boss everyone around…

Cottage industries have been built up – just have a look around an Urbanisation in the morning and you'll see; small vans carrying builders and equipment, units opening to welcome customers and always, always someone with a mop and bucket heading off for a 'changeover.'

We should be proud to be Brits abroad - supporting fellow expats as they try to earn a living in what is not the easiest of environments. It's not always straightforward here for small businesses but the vast majority of expats I've met are hardworking and industrious and get on with things– it's not surprising we need a beer in the evening is it…?

Talking of industrious and inventive there's one person that I'm booking a seat next to come the Armageddon. My mate Charlie can fix anything, and if it can't be fixed – well it's just not worth fixing. This is a man who can get life from a dead battery and his electric from the heavens (although he did get caught and had to disconnect from the pylon up the road), but there is sometimes a pay-off.

He'll repair that old camcorder for you and have it working in no time – the fact that you will need four car batteries with you to now make it run it is a minor inconvenience, but hey! at least it works…

SATURDAY NOVEMBER 27th 2010

Friends, animal lovers, and Americans…lend me your paws would you…and a mop and, by the way, if anyone has found a green flip-flop (size 10) specifically in the Alicante area of Spain – its mine. You see Woopy the Labrador is an early Christmas present from my son (just what I needed, another dog…) and has become part of the family. Lovely as she is…she's also a thief. So my first complaint to K9 animal charity, where we got her from, is that this puppy doesn't do as it's told…at all. When I say come – she goes, and when I tell her to sit…well, there's something lost in translation there I think…but I always clear up. However, my second moan is that I ordered a complete dog, and it appears Woopy isn't. Yes, she's got all her limbs, eyes, fur and teeth – which is more than I can say for my neighbour Pepe, but she only comes with one kidney. I know everyone will say it's ok…she only needs one – it doesn't matter that the other one isn't there. But it's a bit like having a remote control with the Channel 5 button missing – you'd never use it but it's nice to know it's there…

SUNDAY NOVEMBER 28th 2010

More dog trouble came my way today, a gorgeous, sunny winter's afternoon, me putting up a fence in the garden while the dogs soaked up some rays. Then the Guardia Civil turned up. At first it wasn't clear what exactly I'd done wrong to deserve the presence of two officers of the crown at my gate, but here they were.

Apparently someone had crashed into a car and left the scene pretty rapidly, forgetting to fill out the accident form and disappearing into the distance. Apparently, that someone was me.

They asked to see my car, so I showed them.

'No, the other car,' said one of them with very bushy eyebrows (I actually wondered how he could see me but I bet they are handy in the summer…).

I offered the (honest) excuse that I didn't have another but (apparently) I had acquired a BMW (black) with significant frontal damage. It didn't matter what I said they insisted that I must have hidden it somewhere…all this was getting hard to take, especially with his eyebrows moving up and down (like a pair of synchronised caterpillars on a trampoline) as he talked.

Eventually, they agreed to look at my ID and realised that my name, and the guy's they were looking for, were completely different. At last, some common sense was going to prevail (I thought) but I was on another train of thought completely to eyebrows and his mate. My ID was false. It was checked, by phone, by radio; all they failed to do was hold it up to my face and compare but they were not having it. Despite my protestations I was heading for the cooler (I know but it's the only way I can get my name in the same sentence as Steve McQueen...) and arrangements were made (by them) for me to be taken away.

My knights in shining armour turned out to be the Local Police, specifically Paco who arrived in the nick (geddit?) of time and called me 'Dave,'

I almost replied with an 'I love you' as eyebrows whipped his head between the two of us lost in the confusion. My friendly boys in blue began a serious sounding, although I could only hear whispers, the conversation was obviously about me. The looks over the shoulder from all the officers were still unnerving; particularly eyebrows and I began to worry for my future once again. Anyway, to keep a long story long, it turned out that I didn't have a BMW, hadn't crashed and legged it and I was, in fact, the bloke that it said I was. Bit like Ronseal really.

So everyone was happy once again, although eyebrows and co' didn't offer an apology but they did shake my hand over the gate.

It was at that point that Mrs Jones decided to put in an appearance and put her front paws on the top of the gate – eyeballing eyebrows (she was now the same height) – and then it happened.

To give him credit he took it well and returned to his car without another word. Mrs Jones, for her part, had let out the longest belch I've heard from any animal, let alone a Great Dane, into his face. It was compounded by the noise of her cheeks rattling against her gums from the force of the escaping air, and Eyebrows'....er, eyebrows being pushed against his forehead.

I don't expect him to hold a grudge, but just in case, if anyone can bake a nice jam sponge, with a file in it?

Still another evening out with Nicole could make me feel better, I thought. Why am I so thick sometimes?

After chatting away for ages about everything and anything, one of her friends arrived again. This time though the other woman was far from upset and hugged Nicole warmly…before shaking my hand. We chatted for a bit before I asked where her boyfriend was at which point the pair of them started, and then couldn't stop, laughing for ages (which is always fun for the one who hasn't got a clue what they're laughing about isn't it?) until, between sobs of laughter Nicole blurted out, 'didn't you know Noelia (the other girl) is my girlfriend…we've been together for years!'

I found an excuse and left as fast as I could, gutted. I felt like a tortoise that has been banging away for hours only to get off and realise that he's just been making love to a German soldier's helmet… I arrived home and Mitch asked what the matter was. I went into huge detail and told him how I felt about Nicole and then what had happened earlier in the evening… then the laughing started again…git.

MONDAY NOVEMBER 29th 2010

I awoke to the rhythmic patter of sandals on tarmac once again as Bertie and Wooshter made their way to my door. Clearly my 'revelation' last time that I'd already been married twice after they'd lectured on the 'sanctity of marriage' had been forgiven and they were back. I'd forgiven them too (not for any particular reason…but it confused them) and we chatted about everything but Jesus…even though he had a birthday coming up.

They were on good form and kept well clear of the subject of dying – to the point that they were enthusing on the joys of the Garden of Eden.

'That's a coincidence!' I said to them. 'Because on Christmas day I'll be smoking something from the Garden of Eden Café in Holland'.

They left, smiling politely at my attempt at humour.

153

WEDNESDAY DECEMBER 1st 2010

A good morning; this smart-arse editor and his son, Mitch, qualified as Open Water divers and are now enjoying the freedom and beauty of swimming beneath the waves. Under the watchful tutorage of a Course Director – who asked me to mention that teaching me was like trying to hammer cheese into a brick wall –we've completed the exams, the dives and the skills and somehow proved to him that we are capable divers.

It was turning into a good day...and then came the emails.

Very professional and formal at first they held the details for Jeff's (one of the guys who sold for me) salary claim for his last month's wages and expenses. Suffice to say that Arthur C Clarke would have been proud of that creation and I considerably cut the highest wage claim he had ever put in (remember this was our worst month *ever*) but paid what he was really owed.

Then the funny stuff started. If I didn't pay everything that he'd demanded he would go to our competition and the taxman (to drop us in it for having some cash-only clients) and that this was one person 'who you've abused too often...' he was going to bring everything down on top of me and then some. This time I didn't bother with the 'get on with it' bit and told him to just fuck off.

FRIDAY DECEMBER 10th 2010

Freezing cold last night (it was down to 11 degrees...) I headed outside shivering but was soon warmed up by a rude awakening – jumping out of my skin as I took the rubbish out and lifted the lid of the big grey bin to discover a toothless Moro grinning back at me. He was inside (with a miners torch on his head) and after a quick 'hola' he was back to it – head down, and rummaging, - so I turned my attention to the adjacent bin, where a lot of noise was also coming from. I found his wife scouring the bags for her particular brand of treasure…and another toothless smile – complemented with a cheery 'Merry Christmas!' then she was back to it… I love Spain…

What a day. Six weeks after the hearing and full custody of my son granted in my favour, the bill came. Six hundred and fifty Euros more than he had told me in the first place. When I questioned him he told me that they were for court charges that you never know exactly how much they are going to be, until they arrive. His argument for not telling me was precisely that – he didn't know how much they would be. My argument was that he should have warned me, and that he was a prick. I still think the same and he's still my lawyer…that just shows how bad the rest are.

While I was waiting for the case to get to court I, as you would expect, had to make several trips to the lawyer's offices. Maria, the girl on reception, had a mouth like a foghorn (but without the subtleness). She was with a client when I arrived so I waited, in the same room, as she read out his personal life in manner that would have made Reverend Ian Paisley proud. Finally she'd finished with him and as he left I gave him a shrug as if to say 'never mind mate,' but he just looked like he'd stepped out of a wind tunnel.

As I sat Maria immediately blasted, 'your wife' (which she pronounced 'wayif' because she was talking so loud) but I held my hand up and told her that, strange as it may seem I didn't want the rest of the office (or anyone within her voice range i.e. Italy) to hear about my personal life. She shrugged and sent me in to see the lawyer, who after hearing my complaint, shrugged and said,

'But that's how we always do it.'

I shrugged back…and said 'yes, I know…cos you're shit…'

I rest my case.

When it comes to Christmas in Spain, things are a little different to the UK. Out come the usual Spanish decorations, 'Jesus weeping on a cross' or 'Mary holding the infant child…and weeping' or even 'the three shepherds looking down on the saviour' and they're bawling their eyes out too! What a miserable sight at what, these days, is expected to be a happy time of the year.

You see the Spanish still hold on to the idea that Christmas is all about the Lord, Jesus wotsit – our saviour etc. They haven't quite caught on to the concept of the 25th of December, and the days surrounding it, being all about having fun, giving prezzies, eating loads (the exception) and doing something wholly inappropriate that will require the rest of the year for the other half to forgive you.

Long gone are the days of putting on your Sunday best and popping down to the local church, to eat some bread or whatever it is they do there, and then arriving home to eat a full roast before dropping asleep in front of Her Maj (bless her). These days we still worship and pray for the arrival of our saviour, but now it is a rather fat bloke in a funny red suit, rather than the king of the Jews. Ask any kid under the age of twenty five what is the best thing about Christmas and they won't be stressing the need for a few moments thought during the day to remember our lord – they'll be blasting Nicholas Cage's head to smithereens on the X-box while asking 'has Santa been yet?'

Mark my words, it won't be long before the supposed birthday of Jesus Christ will be only known as the day that Father Christmas makes his incredible journey around the world delivering presents at the speed of light – and that *is* something to admire. And he had a reindeer with a neon nose – all Mary and Joseph can offer is a pretty shabby looking donkey.

The Spanish are gradually moving that way too, their traditional day for receiving presents is the 6th of January (Dia de Reyes) but over the last ten years I've noticed that many families are now dishing out the goodies on the 25th of December. Now that could be because they believe that the 25th truly is the day to honour the lord or….it could be to shut the kids up.

And if that doesn't reinforce my argument about FC taking over from JC then the fact that fewer people go to church over Christmas than ever before should do. It's a true fact that the number of worshippers that do now get on their knees in front of a priest (insert your own joke here) during this period is still not enough to fill two of the 50 or so football stadiums that will be packed on Boxing Day...worshipping football.

Spain is not Oxford Street at Christmas it's more like your Nan's when you went for a visit and she's shoved a tree on the coffee table because she thinks she ought to, but it's going the right way, in my opinion, Christmas is about fun, religion doesn't seem to be..

Next time I'll be focusing on that other icon that we think of when it comes to religious festivities…the Easter Bunny.

That's it, a year in my life – and that of several others. I'm not sure if mine is a fairly typical expat life – but what you've read really happened, it's all true. That's why I love this place and the things that happen every single day - it's always interesting. But the running theme throughout this book is that Spain is different…let me explain…

When all is said and done the only real difference in Spain is us and it's how we look at the country that's different to the natives. We want the sunshine, the relaxed, Mediterranean way of life, we even adopt the 'mañana' idea of putting things off, but what we really want is all that but in a nice efficient bundle that means that things get done without having to visit ten offices and get fifteen bits of paper stamped. But then this wouldn't be Spain.

Those of us who came to Spain to live, and are still here after a good while, have gotten used to it, we go with the flow because Spain ain't gonna change for us. It will change in its own good time but for now we should enjoy it for what it is and when the US version of a western lifestyle finally creeps over the border, this place will be much the poorer for it.

Long may Spain resist the 'need to change' and may its people continue to have three hours break in the afternoon. May they continue to find every possible reason to have a day off and fill the day with a celebration – with their family.

Spain is (arguably) behind the times in many ways and I think, at the end of the day, that is what we really like about the place. When people moan that Spain is 30 years behind the rest of the world we tend to forget that not so long ago, when we lived in our native countries, we wished for things to be as they were thirty years ago.

They won't be rushed, they won't be hurried. It's like trying to make a kid walk faster when they're not happy – you give 'em a little shove and they take no notice at all, often going even slower.

It's their country, their rules – whether they are written in stone or just the way things are always done - no amount of threats, screaming and shouting will change any of that, and (mostly) those of us who choose to live here are content with that.

Whole areas of this country are inhabited by expats. Mallorca is virtually run by the Germans who have half a regiment on the town council and towns such as Torrevieja on the Costa Blanca have areas where, if you wanted to, you could spend the whole of your time not speaking Spanish. And, in general, our hosts accept it and get on with us, and it.

If you're reading this and thinking of moving abroad do yourself a favour and get to know the cultural and traditional roots and routines, it'll open up a whole new world and, trust me, you'll have a great time in a beautiful place.

Thanks for listening, Dave x

SPAIN…
An overview

DRIVING
Nothing exists if they have to move their head to see it.
They stand at zebra crossings and don't cross
They park on Zebra crossings so YOU can't cross.
If you step onto the crossing thinking they will stop – they won't.
Any car will fit in any space…given time and a decent set of bumpers.
If car can't get into said space – park it half in with the hazards on.
They don't indicate
The best place for rubbish is out of the car window
The car should be parked as close to the shop/supermarket/bar as is physically possible – use of the curb is the norm but walking distance must be kept to an absolute minimum.
Asking a policeman the way is met with 'you'd be better off asking someone who has lived here longer'

WALKING (like driving - but slower…)
Conversations need to be held on the narrowest part of the pavement at the highest volume possible.
Stopping abruptly - foreigners habitually pile into the back of them which is then met with a huff.

BANK

Your bank will take the money out of your account if it is owed to them (pension, mortgage, etc.) and then send you a text telling you that you are overdrawn…

They answer the phone when you're queuing in the bank, and chat for ages.

They don't answer the phone when you're calling…or they ask you to call back.

SHOPPING

They've lived here longer…therefore queues are for YOU not them.

If it's not on show – they haven't got it.

All joints of meat must be chopped into tiny pieces before being handed over by the butcher.

How the hell should a supermarket assistant know where stuff is kept?

When you go to get the new TV and have persuaded the wife about a plasma screen - and its ability to change your life – remember that Jose, your assistant, was probably selling coffees yesterday.

You may have ordered a red one but a blue has arrived…take it away – you ordered it.

If you say you need it for Tuesday – it'll be here Tuesday… maybe.

Phones, mates & children all have a priority over you.

You have your rights…unless they conflict with the shop assistant's view of things.

You want HOT coffee…?

They are never to blame…ever.

LEGAL

Laws, bye-laws etc. are only applicable to outsiders (depending on policeman- love you Paco).

LIFESTYLE

Dunking a croissant in a cup of coffee is not disgusting
Spitting is not disgusting
Killing a Bull for fun is not disgusting

p.s. Telefonica are bastards…

Dave Bull

ABOUT THE AUTHOR

Dave Bull has been living and working in Spain since 2000. Now a full-time writer he lives with his son, Mitch and two dogs on the Costa Blanca penning his experiences and observations on living life as an expat in Spain.

Always from his own 'different' perspective, he publishes one of the most successful magazines on the Costa Blanca and has been the Editor of two regional expat newspapers.

Clearly not professionally trained as a writer, if you really have nothing better to do, have a read, (and a laugh) about Dave's experiences at the hands of the Spanish - where he reveals, as ever, in his own unique style just what some of us expats get up to in Spain.

Having had his own radio shows and now touring with his 'One Man Show' he is well known on the Costa Blanca and becoming a recognised name throughout the expat community in Spain and beyond.

Read more at:
www.loadofbull.es

Dave Bull

Printed in Great Britain
by Amazon